This is an important new book about human motivation, about the reasons people have for their actions. What is distinctively new about it is its focus on how people see or understand their situations, options, and prospects. By taking account of people's understandings (along with their beliefs and desires), Professor Schick is able to expand the current theory of decision and action.

The author provides a perspective on the topic by outlining its history. He defends his new theory against criticism, considers its formal structure, and shows at length how it resolves many currently debated problems: the problems of conflict and weakness of will, Allais' problem, Kahneman and Tversky's problems, Newcomb's problem, and others.

This book will be of special interest to philosophers, psychologists, and economists.

UNDERSTANDING ACTION

Understanding Action

An Essay on Reasons

FREDERIC SCHICK

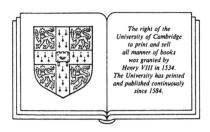

The right of the
University of Cambridge
to print and sell
all manner of books
was granted by
Henry VIII in 1534.
The University has printed
and published continuously
since 1584.

CAMBRIDGE UNIVERSITY PRESS

Cambridge

New York   Port Chester   Melbourne   Sydney

CAMBRIDGE UNIVERSITY PRESS
Cambridge, New York, Melbourne, Madrid, Cape Town, Singapore, São Paulo

Cambridge University Press
The Edinburgh Building, Cambridge CB2 8RU, UK

Published in the United States of America by Cambridge University Press, New York

www.cambridge.org
Information on this title: www.cambridge.org/9780521403306

First published 1991

A catalogue record for this publication is available from the British Library

Library of Congress Cataloguing in Publication data
Schick, Frederic, 1929–
Understanding action : an essay on reasons / Frederic Schick.
p. cm.
Includes index.
ISBN 0-521-40330-8. – ISBN 0-521-40886-5 (pbk.)
1. Act (Philosophy) 2. Motivation (Psychology) 3. Decision –
making. 4. Comprehension. I. Title.
B105.A35S35 1991
128′.4 – dc20 91-9146
CIP

ISBN 978-0-521-40330-6 hardback
ISBN 978-0-521-40886-8 paperback

Transferred to digital printing 2007

for Kay, again

CONTENTS

Contents

1

INTRODUCTION

1.1 A CHANGE OF HEART

WRITING about his experiences in the Spanish Civil War, George Orwell tells this story. He had gone out to a spot near the Fascist trenches from which he thought he might snipe at someone. He waited a long time without any luck. None of the enemy made an appearance. Then, at last, some disturbance took place, much shouting and blowing of whistles followed, and a man

> . . . jumped out of the trench and ran along the parapet in full view. He was half-dressed and was holding up his trousers with both hands as he ran. I refrained from shooting at him. . . . I did not shoot partly because of that detail about the trousers. I had come here to shoot at "Fascists"; but a man holding up his trousers isn't a "Fascist," he is visibly a fellow-creature, similar to yourself, and you don't feel like shooting at him.[1]

Why did Orwell put down his gun? We have a general theory of action that ought to be of use to us here. The theory says that people's actions issue from their beliefs and desires, that to explain what someone did we need to know only what he believed and what he wanted. Suppose that some person wanted *this* and believed that to get it he had to do *that*. The belief and the desire together were his reason, and the reasons a person has lead him to do what he does.

---

1 George Orwell, "Looking Back on the Spanish Civil War," in *A Collection of Essays* (Garden City: Doubleday, 1957), p. 199.

Orwell's story doesn't fit this mold. As Orwell tells it, he was ready to shoot. What he believed and what he wanted prompted him to do it, and he would in fact have fired if the man's trousers hadn't been down. Yet seeing the man half naked changed no beliefs that Orwell had. He had known all along that, under their pants, Fascists were like himself, that they were "fellow creatures." Nor did it change what he wanted. He had not wanted to shoot fellow creatures and he didn't now cease to want to shoot Fascists. But if his beliefs and desires were such as to lead him to shoot if it weren't for those pants, some other factor, neither a belief nor a desire, must be brought in to explain why he didn't. His reason for refraining from shooting can't just have been some belief and desire.

Orwell admits that his behavior may be puzzling, and so he comments on it. It wasn't the detail about the dropped trousers that stopped him but what that detail revealed. He says he had wanted to bring down a Fascist but that "a man holding up his trousers isn't a 'Fascist.' " This would make no sense at all but for those inside quotes – these are seen-in-this-way markers and they tell the story. Of course the man up ahead was a Fascist, but with his buttocks flapping as he ran, he couldn't be *seen* as a Fascist. At least he couldn't be seen as a Fascist by Orwell, so Orwell reports. Flushed from his trench without any warning, the man was caught with his ideology down and was "visibly" a fellow creature. The Fascist half naked was "visibly" human. His personhood trumped his politics.

The question is, what stayed Orwell's hand? A part of the answer may be clear enough. He had formed a new understanding of what he would have been doing. He now saw his shooting that soldier as firing a gun at a fellow human. Yes, but how did that new understanding connect with the beliefs and desires he had? And how did it block the action he says he had been waiting to take?

We will put these matters off. Let me here say only that Orwell's story is not unique. Many other wartime memoirs

2

speak of similar experiences.[2] Nor does this sort of thing happen only in war and on battlefields. The new understanding or "seeing" needn't even be of any other person. Here are some lines from a recollection of village life in Victorian England. The author is speaking of his boyhood days:

> We loved to go down into that . . . [sawpit]. It was always moist and cool; there was a perpetual odor of sawdust, and large yellow frogs often peered out at us from chinks in its slab-lined walls. Once . . . I saw a large frog, seated on its haunches, staring at me. . . . With the thoughtlessness common to boys, I raised a stick to strike it, when instantly it covered its eyes with its hands, as though dreading to see the blow that it was powerless to avert. The act was so unexpected and surprising, so truly human in character, that I was at once ashamed, and dropped my stick.[3]

The boy had wanted to hit a target and it may be he still wanted this. But a frog hiding its face in fear can't be seen as just a target. It is "visibly a fellow creature, similar to yourself," and you don't feel like hitting it.

1.2 A DIFFICULT CHOICE

These stories speak of self-restraint. They speak of a person being deflected from a harsh purpose he had. The person involved is shown to be turning from coldness of heart to compassion. It sometimes happens the opposite way. Say that the soldier in Orwell's report, not knowing he was seen, stopped to pull up his pants. Suppose he went on to button his tunic. This had the Fascist insignia on it, and that brought Orwell, hidden and watching, back to the fact that the man was an enemy. It called him back to the duties of war, and he took aim and fired.

2 Michael Walzer discusses some cases; see his *Just and Unjust Wars* (New York: Basic Books, 1977), pp. 138–43.
3 Walter Rose, *The Village Carpenter* (New York: New Amsterdam Books, 1988), p. 3.

The motive factor in this hypothetical story is of the same sort as that above: a sudden recall to a neglected truth, a reminder of something known all along, a refocusing of attention.

Or take a very different situation. Here neither restraint nor letting go is at issue, nor any grasp of the fellow-personhood of some other. The report is by Jean-Paul Sartre and is about a young man Sartre knew during the German occupation of France:

> His father was quarreling with his mother and was also in-
> clined to be a "collaborator"; his elder brother had been killed
> in the German offensive of 1940 and this young man, with a
> sentiment somewhat primitive but generous, burned to avenge
> him. His mother was living alone with him, deeply afflicted by
> the semi-treason of his father and by the death of her eldest
> son, and her only consolation was in this young man. But he,
> at this moment, had the choice between going to England to
> join the Free French Forces or of staying near his mother and
> helping her to live. . . . Consequently, he found himself con-
> fronted by two very different modes of action. . . . He had to
> choose between these two.[4]

What course the man took Sartre does not say. Nor does he say what prompted that choice, what led him to do what he did. It could have been some new information, some change in the man's beliefs. He might have learned about the generals' squab-bles or about their defeats in the field. That might have led him to lose faith in their army and so to look elsewhere to avenge his brother. Or he might have learned that his father was not a collaborator but a double agent, working at great risk for the Allies, and that his mother knew it and only pretended to be in despair in order to shield her husband, that indeed she was devoted to him and did not depend on her son at all. Learning this would have freed the young man and allowed him to leave with an easy conscience. Perhaps it did happen in such a way,

4 Jean-Paul Sartre, *Existentialism and Humanism* (London: Eyre Methuen, 1948), pp. 35–6.

but it needn't have happened so. What this person did in the end needn't have issued from any change in his beliefs.

Nor need there have been any change in his interests, in what the young man wanted. He wanted to join the army and also to stay with his mother, and it may be that this remained firm. Even after he did what he did, he may still have wished he could have also done the other. Again we can make up stories, but again too, they needn't be true; nothing like that need have happened. Still, what sense could we make of this? If neither his beliefs nor his desires had changed, how did he come to decide what to do? How did he shift into action?

It may have happened like this. He woke up one morning to the sound of marching and of unfamiliar music. Some German soldiers were tramping by in the street, singing a German song. It struck him that while his country's enemies were parading their triumph, he was lying in bed. He then saw his staying at home as a sort of spinelessness. How different this shameful life of his was from that of his friends in the army! He resolved at that moment to join them.

Or perhaps this happened instead. He spoke to his mother one day of leaving. She said not a word, but her face went blank. She looked like a frightened child. He saw that his leaving her as she then was would be an act of abandonment. That jolted him, and it made up his mind.

In both scenarios, what eases the quandary is a sort of conversion. No new belief or desire enters but rather a new understanding of the situation. We may assume, in our sleeping-late story, that the man always knew he was passive. He had known it from the start but had never faced up to it. He had known too that joining the army was a patriotic obligation for him, but never before had that sunk in either, never before had he *seen* it that way.

Likewise in the second story. The man had of course known all along that joining the army meant leaving his mother, but never before had he seen his departure as an act of abandonment. Never before had he seen his staying as his filial duty. When he finally did see it so, his problem of what he should do was settled. It was the way he then saw things that did it, or his coming to have this new view – his conversion to it.

So it had been for Orwell. The sight of the soldier's nakedness awakened in Orwell a sense of his kinship. It led him to understand shooting the man as a kind of betrayal. Here the conversion had been to a new understanding of his shooting that man. But my point goes beyond Orwell's case, and beyond Sartre's too. It is meant to be general. The point is that a person's conduct doesn't derive from his beliefs and desires only. Sometimes a basic factor is how he understands some event or situation, how he has come to *see* it. In such a case, to explain what he does, we must bring out this factor.

1.3 WHAT THIS BOOK IS ABOUT

A person may come to understand that he himself is a human being – or even that he is naked. The news may hit home with a jolt. After Adam and Eve ate the forbidden fruit, "the eyes of them both were opened, and they knew that they were naked; and they sewed fig leaves together, and made themselves aprons."[5] The medieval commentator Rashi exclaims, "Even a blind person knows when he is naked! What then does 'and they knew that they were naked' signify?"[6] This is just the sort of question we will be asking here.

Their coming to see that they were naked led Adam and Eve to make a big change; it led them to put on clothes. But the factor of understanding plays a role too where all stays the same. Orwell had often fired at Fascists – that had long ceased to be something new. On none of these many other occasions had he

---

5 Genesis 3:7.
6 *Pentateuch with Rashi's Commentary*, Vol. 1 (London: Shapiro and Vallentine, 1929), p. 13.

wanted to kill human beings, and of course he believed (he *knew*) that Fascists were human beings. He put their humanity out of mind. He focused on their being Fascists, and it was this that let him shoot. Without a grasp of how he then saw things, we can't account for his life as a soldier. We can't explain his usual conduct untroubled by qualms about killing people any more than we can explain his special restraint on that day.

So the cases above may mislead. We need to bring out the seeings factor not only where someone's habits give way or where he is moved to some change. We need to find it also in his reasons for staying the course, for persisting. It figures not only in explanations of the collapse of a marriage but also where we try to explain why a husband or wife stuck it out. Indeed, it figures fully as much where the marriage in question was happy, though how it figures there is obvious. No need to remark that a person sees *not* walking out as preserving the marriage. The obvious goes without saying, but it is there nonetheless.

What is this special sort of understanding to which we are calling attention? What is a cognitive *seeing* of a situation? ("What does 'they saw that *x*' signify?") How is it related to believing and wanting and through them to actual conduct? These are not mainstream philosophical questions, but there are people who have written about them, or about others that are closely related. Aristotle spoke of the role of a person's view (his "grasp") of his options of conduct. Kant did the same in his ethics, and so did some lesser historical figures. In his theory of knowledge, Kant held that seeing or understanding ("judgment") must enter to tell us how to apply what we know – he spoke of the "faculty of subsuming under rules" – and this idea finds an echo in our own century in the writings of Wittgenstein. We will want to consider some of these different ideas and approaches.

Other questions will then come up. The point to be made is that people's understandings are a major factor of what it is that moves them, that how they see their options and prospects plays a central causal role. How does this bear on the usual theory, that of belief-and-desire reasons? Would allowing for understandings avoid the problems that trouble that theory? Could it account for the results obtained in the experiments that have been run? And is the way things are seen or understood subject to any standards: can we see things rightly or wrongly, are there *improper* understandings? These questions will be taken up in Chapters 3, 4, and 5.

What follows is about the motivation of action, about the reasons that people have. The study of human motivation is known as the study of *practical reason*. It has a very long history, and the next chapter will survey that. This will be done rather briskly, with no pretension to scholarship. The purpose will be to get some perspective on the subject as we now have it so that we can later remark on how our theory departs from the usual. Since the history we want to lay out has largely ignored the questions just raised, in this next chapter these questions are shelved. Toward the end of Chapter 2, we will consider how what preceded can be defended against certain critics and also what formal structure it has. In Chapter 3, we then get down to business. There we consider what might be done to expand on the current theory: we ask how that theory might be revised to allow for people's seeings or understandings.

2

PRACTICAL REASON

2.1 IN THE BEGINNING

THE history of the theory of practical reason begins with some questions by Aristotle. How does it happen that "sometimes thinking is accompanied by action and sometimes not?"[1] Aristotle notes that this question is similar to one we might ask about pure speculation, speculation about what things are like. In that, we draw a new belief from some others we have – that is, we do this where we conclude. Why do we sometimes conclude a reasoning and sometimes come to no conclusion? He suggests that this has to do with the pattern of the reasoning involved. It has to do with whether the reasoning reflects a proper argument form, the logic of speculative-argument forms being worked out in his theory of the syllogism. In a practical context too, all depends on the pattern of the argument, though there is the fundamental difference that

> ... [what] results from the ... premises is ... [an] action. For example, whenever someone thinks that every man should take walks, and that he is a man, at once he takes a walk. Or if he thinks that no man should take a walk now, and that he is a man, at once he remains at rest. And he does both of these things if nothing prevents or compels him. I should make something good; a house is something good. At once he makes a house. I need covering; a cloak is a covering. I need a cloak. What I need, I have to make; I need a cloak. I have to make a cloak. And the conclusion, the "I have to make a cloak," is an action.[2]

1 Aristotle, *De Motu Animalium*, 701a.   2 Ibid.

9

As examples of reasoning, these are certainly odd. Still, there is a plausible thesis being presented in them. The passage proposes an answer to Aristotle's question about thinking and action. When does thinking lead to action? Thinking makes for action where the thinking is of a certain sort and connects with the agent's desires. More fully, the agent takes a certain action where he believes it is open to him and that his acting this way is required for something else, and he wants that other thing.

The passage sketches some practical inferences, reasonings leading to action, and it suggests that the premises of such inferences always are of two sorts. The premises bring out the agent's reasons, and so we might say that a person's reasons always have two sorts of components. I shall be speaking of beliefs and desires. Aristotle describes the first component (the belief part) as *thinking* or *knowing*. The second (desire) component he describes as *wanting* or *needing* or as what *should* be done – "I should make something good." (He sometimes speaks of *thinking* here too; "thinking" is then a catch-all for him.)

The inference or reasoning to which this refers needn't extend over time. There need be no lengthy deliberation, no nervous pacing of the soul. I want a certain something, I think this requires my doing *that,* and I now do it, all in a flash. No pause for reflection here. Where my believing and wanting move me, they may move me slowly or quickly. I may reflect on the movement or not. It may be conscious and fully monitored or impulsive or even unaware.

Suppose I now act on some reason or other. I will later search out that reason if I ask why I acted as I did. If I am asking about someone else, I will look for just this about him – I will look for the reason he had. So we have in a theory of reasons a part of a model of the explanation of action. For Aristotle, it comes to this, that to explain what someone did, we need to point out what this person wanted and what he thought he could do about it. Putting the theory formally: where a person wants x to be true and believes that x requires y (or presupposes it or is in part realized by it) and that he might now bring about *y*, he now brings it about. The desire and belief he has in the case are the reason he has for *y*'ing. And where we know a person's reason, we have (a part of) an explanation of what he did.

The reader may object that many actions have no reasons. We blink, we yawn, we hiccup. No doubt these things we do are caused, but their causes are physical only; beliefs and desires don't enter. We have no reasons for yawning and the rest, so these doings cannot be explained by bringing out any reasons.

Aristotle would say in response that beliefs and desires are here thought of too narrowly. The desire component of an agent's reason refers to some purpose he has. In the case of a blink of an eye, that is often to moisten its surface. A purpose needn't be conscious. Likewise, a belief may be merely instinctive, not only in animals but also in humans. A bird knows that to build a nest it must collect some twigs, that safety calls for taking flight, etc. That is then what it *believes*. Thus too, we know (and so *believe*) that to moisten our eyes we must blink. On this broad conception of beliefs and desires, every action does have a reason.

Let us go back to Aristotle's examples; these don't all square with our reading of the text.[3] Take the one about building a house: "I should make something good; a house is something good. At once he makes a house." As a piece of reasoning, this is not very solid. All right, I'll make something good, but why precisely a house? And how could anyone explain what I did if he knew only how I reasoned here? This is not a serious problem. We need to consider the circumstances; perhaps I think that building houses is the only thing I can do. This belief about myself then contributes to my reason (if I am to do something good, it will have to be a house), and the reasoning does have force.

What is more troubling is that we are sometimes offered what look like very different cases. Aristotle then puts it like this: "We

3 The reading follows that of Martha Nussbaum in her *Aristotle's De Motu Animalium* (Princeton: Princeton University Press, 1978), Essay 4.

debate not about ends but about means. For a doctor does not deliberate whether he shall heal, nor an orator whether he shall persuade, nor a statesman whether he shall produce law and order. . . . They assume the end and consider how and by what means it is to be attained. . . . "4 These people want some *x* and believe that some *y* would establish (or produce or lead to) *x*. They believe too they might bring about *y*. On these grounds, they bring *y* about. Here it is thought that *x* would hold if *y* were to hold. In the model sketched above, *x* would hold *only* if *y* did. Here it is thought that *y* is (or would be) a sufficient condition of *x;* above, *y* is thought to be *necessary* for *x*. Do we need a second model to cover the sufficient-condition cases?

A question here comes up very like the one that came up in the house builder's story. There it was, why precisely a house? Here it is, why precisely these means? But here we are left in no doubt. The passage just quoted continues: "and if [the end] seems to be produced by several means they [the agents] consider by which it is most easily and best produced. . . . " Why will the easiest or best means be taken? The answer to that is obvious. People don't want just to attain certain ends; they want to attain them in some suitable way, in the "most easily and best produced" way. But this returns us to our first model. If a person wants to get something in the most suitable way – let his getting it so be *x* – and he thinks that *y* is that way, then he thinks that *y* is not only a sufficient but also a necessary condition of *x*. The means-end cases thus fall into line; they are covered by our basic theory. In these cases too the agent brings about what he thinks is a necessary condition of what he wants.

One detail of most of the examples presented calls for special attention. There is a suggestion in them of some impulse going from the premises to the conclusion. The agent is repeatedly said to act "at once" in the way the premises require. The usual reading is that Aristotle holds that the action follows from its

4 *Nichomachean Ethics,* 1112b.

12

premises by some sort of necessity, that the agent whose premises they are *must* now act accordingly. The logical force of a speculative inference derives from that of the syllogism it expresses. A practical inference is compelling too, though in a different way.

This idea has been much discussed, and usually Aristotle has been faulted for it. If he thought that a practical reasoning was deductively valid, he was certainly wrong. The premises of such reasonings are reports of certain beliefs and desires. The conclusions, he says, are actions. How could there be a deductive structure connecting such disparate elements? How can any mere logic say that people always act on their reasons?

Aristotle knew his logic, so it's not likely he thought it said this. What then could he have meant when he spoke of what a person *must* do? Working it through in modern terms, we can hazard a guess. Most modern philosophical analyses of explanation require explanations to be deductive. They hold that in order to explain what happened we have to show that it *had* to happen, given the total circumstances. The report that is given of an event's occurrence must logically follow from the report of what explains it: the *explanandum* must follow from the *explanans*. The idea that explanation involves entailment doubtless has very old roots. It may be that they go back to the Greeks, that Aristotle himself had some such idea. If so, what he said here makes good sense, that a person's reason explains his action only where a report of that reason *plus* a report of the circumstances entails some report of that action. But what in a person's circumstances could be drawn in to complete the entailment?

Consider the relation of my believing x and also believing that x-only-if-y to my believing y. From x and x-only-if-y together, y follows by simple deduction. Still, my believing y does not follow from my having the other beliefs: I may believe both x and x-only-if-y and yet not believe y. My beliefs are then not deductively *closed*. Suppose now that my beliefs *are* closed, or at least closed in this instance, that I do believe y, and moreover that I believe it *because* it follows from some other items I believe. That is, I have these latter beliefs, and "a single opinion results from the two,"[5] or again, "whenever [I] think the two premises, [I] think and put together the conclusion,"[6] my outcome belief "resulting" from the beliefs with which I here started. Let me say, if this is true, that I am deductively *driven* in this instance. From my believing both x and *x-only-if-y plus* my being deductively driven it logically follows that I believe y – this by the definition of *drivenness*.

The principle of deductive closure can be stretched to cover more than beliefs. It can be held to require that, if I *want* both x and y and if z follows from these two together, I now also want z. It can be held to require yet further that, if I believe x and want y, and if z follows from *x-and-y*, I also want z (we will touch this up later). This third idea of closure cites some constraints imposed by beliefs and desires jointly, and there is a corresponding extension of the idea of deductive drivenness. On that extended concept, from my believing x and wanting y and *x-and-y*'s implying z *plus* my being deductively driven it logically follows that I want z. (Here I don't just want z but want it *because* of the rest.)

But how do we get from wanting z to acting so as to make it true? Our wanting something does not imply our bringing that something about. But suppose the agent to be *unimpeded* in this special sense, that what he wants and thinks he can bring about, he does now bring about, and brings about because of this belief and desire he has. No hindrance or restraint or disability stops him. As Aristotle puts it, "nothing prevents or compels him [to do the opposite],"[7] so his wantings flow right into action. His acting follows by definition, by the definition of being *unimpeded:* from someone's wanting z and believing that he can bring

5 Ibid., 1147a.   6 Aristotle, *De Motu Animalium*, 701a.   7 Ibid.

14

it about *plus* his here being unimpeded it logically follows that he brings it about.

A deductively *driven* person is one who not only abides by logic but governs his beliefs and desires by it. An *unimpeded* person is one who goes for what he wants and thinks he can get. No one, of course, is driven or unimpeded in every context and all the time, but a person may be one or both in this or that situation. Where a person is driven or unimpeded, that does not enter any reasons he has. This because reasons are causes of actions, and drivenness and unimpededness are not causal factors. We might describe them as *meta*causal: they are states of the agent revealing what it is that causally moves him.

Let us say of someone who is both driven and unimpeded in some situation that he is *effective* there. This makes it true by definition that a (currently) effective person does what he has a reason for doing. From just the fact that he has this reason it does not follow that he now acts, but his acting follows from that plus his effectiveness in the case. What it comes to is that a person who is effective must act on his reasons – must necessarily act on them – that such a person's reasons determine what he does.

So we get back to the thesis of a reason's having logical force. We can't (and needn't) accept the idea that reasons suffice for explanation, but something very similar turns out to be a tautology. Its being a tautology does not hold against it. A tautology cannot explain what happens; only facts can explain. But the new tautologous thesis isn't meant to be part of any explanans. It says about certain explanantia that they have logical force, that statements reporting the agent's reasons *plus* his being effective have such force. This is indeed a tautology, but it doesn't figure in any explanans of any explanation. No part of any explanans is itself claimed to be tautological.

Aristotle may have been thinking of something like the above. He suggests at several points that the agent to whom he refers is

15

driven and unimpeded, that he is being effective. Then again, this may have him wrong. He wanted his analysis to apply to animals as well as to human beings, and it is hard to think of a dog as being deductively driven. Still, whether or not he meant the above, we can (and will) make use of it here, where only people concern us. Once more, since a reason entails an action only along with effectiveness, that the agent had this reason does not itself explain what he did. His having this reason *plus* his being effective does however give us an explanation.

It isn't enough for an explanandum to follow from its explanans; another condition must be met too. If we ask how come there is a cobra lurking under the bed, it won't content us to be told that there are *two* cobras there. The latter implies the former, but it doesn't explain it. We want to know how that cobra got there, to have our sense of anomaly lifted. We want to connect that unlikely cobra with how such things always go. This means that we need some generalization that covers the case – some general law of nature. On Aristotle's theory, as it is usually put, there are no laws in explanantia of action, only reports of beliefs and desires. So, as it stands, his theory falls short.

Our amplified Aristotelianism gives us the generality we need, for drivenness and unimpededness speak of causal links. Again, these states are not causes themselves, but they refer to the causal sources of what the agent wants or what he does, and on the familiar Humean analysis, a cause implies a general truth. On that analysis, *a* causes *b* only if that is how things always go, only if *a*'s are followed by *b*'s in situations like these. The conduct of a person who is driven and unimpeded is thus covered by general laws, and these laws are implicitly present in every explanans that describes him that way. Aristotle himself was no Humean. His own idea of causation was different, so an authentic Aristotelian still has a problem here. But if we move beyond Aristotle and read his theory as Hume might have done, the theory he offers is workable.

We could adopt a different theory. Instead of making the agent's effectiveness a separate component of all explanantia of action, we could build the causation of his actions directly into the definition of his reasons – modern theories often do this.[8] Let the explanans of some action say that a certain belief-and-desire was the agent's reason in the case. Both the requirement that the explanandum must follow and the requirement that it follows from a generalization would be met. But, on this line, a belief-and-desire that *isn't* effective would not be a reason. Keeping causation extrinsic to reasons allows both for reasons that are acted upon and for those that are not.

I have presented some basic features of the Aristotelian theory. As far as these go, it is not controversial; that is, all students of practical reason accept either it or something like it. Not so with what the above leaves out. This part not yet mentioned played no role at all in the later development of the theory, and the analysis we have today is, I believe, the worse for it. But no need to speak of that now. We will keep to the usual line in the rest of this chapter. We will return in the next to put the missing factor back into place.

2.2 UNCERTAINTY

Here is Aristotle again, reporting the thinking of a doctor:

> ... [S]ince *this* is health, if the subject is to be healthy *this* must first be present, e.g., a uniform state of body, and if this is to be present, there must be heat; and the physician goes on thinking thus until he reduces the matter to a final something which he himself can produce.[9]

---

8 See, for instance, Donald Davidson's "Actions, Reasons, and Causes" in his *Essays on Actions and Events* (Oxford: Oxford University Press, 1980). See also Alvin I. Goldman, *A Theory of Human Action* (New York: Prentice-Hall, 1979), esp. pp. 72ff.

9 Aristotle, *Metaphysics*, 1032b.

This line of thinking fits in well with the theory of reasons above. The doctor wants his patient to recover. Since he thinks that requires some action he believes he might now take, he now wants to take it. And so he now takes that action.

No doubt the doctors of ancient Greece often thought and acted this way, but they may also often have reasoned along less confident lines. They were aware that their interventions might do more harm than good. Perhaps the treatment they had in mind would only make things worse. Perhaps it would cure the patient's disease but have some dismal side-effect. There is some evidence that this troubled them then as much as it does their colleagues today. The classical Hippocratic writings reveal a concern with the circumstances of a case, with the patient's habits and his medical history, even with the local climate. Doctors were cautioned to study these matters so as not to be "at a loss in the treatment."[10] A doctor must often have been "at a loss"; he must have often known too little to be sure of what to do.

One can imagine that in such cases the doctor's thinking took account of that. He might then have reasoned like this: "The patient could be of sort m or he could be of sort n. If I now did a and he is of the m-sort, he would quickly get well; but if he is an n, he would die on the spot. If I did b and he is an m, he would get worse; while if he is an n, he would stay as he is. It would be nice if I cured this person and terrible if he died, a sad thing if he stayed as he is, and sadder still if he got worse. In the light of all of this, I will hold my breath and do. . . . "

Aristotle offers no instance of this common sort of thinking. Indeed, he couldn't have found any place for such a reasoning in his system. On the basic Aristotelian theory, only the agent's beliefs and desires have any role to play. The if-then bits in the paragraph above reflect the doctor's beliefs, and clearly the doctor *wants* to help. But how do we fit in the calculations of nice/sad/sadder/terrible? Aristotle may have suspected some

10 Hippocrates, *Airs, Waters, Places*, 2.

problem. In another context he says, "whether this or that shall be enacted is a . . . task requiring calculation; and there must be a single standard to measure by, for that is pursued which is *greater.*"[11] But he offers no "single standard," and he sometimes even dismisses the attempt to discover one.

There is a second problem for him in the issue of what the patient might be like. The patient might be an *m* or an *n*. What does "might be" mean? How should judgments of *mightness* be read? And how do they relate to the issue of the proper treatment of the patient?

Aristotle takes up some questions of *mightness*, of possibility and contingency, but the questions of this sort he studies have no practical bearing. (Take some battle that *might* be fought; is it now either true or false that it will take place? If it is already true, how can that battle be only possible? And if it is already false, is it possible at all?) There is no guidance here for the doctor in the problem he had to face. The doctor knew that, whatever he did, the outcome would hinge on which possibility held. Any one of them might in fact hold; that is what made them all *possible.* Still, some deserved to be taken seriously, and others called for less attention. How ought the doctor to choose what to do?

Let me put it another way. A doctor is bound to learn very quickly that every treatment that offers some promise also involves some risk. Indeed, increasing the promise of helping sometimes increases the risk of harming. In these last cases, where he makes up his mind, the doctor trades off the latter against the former. He wants to take the course that offers the best trade-off he can now get, and he may sometimes find that course by applying some rule of thumb. (If the patient is choking, thump him on the back!) But he cannot reflect on his problem, cannot think at all clearly about it, unless he can think about trade-offs, unless he has the concepts needed for an analysis of them.

11 *De Anima,* 434a.

One such concept is the concept of the desirability of the possible outcomes. This is the "common standard" that Aristotle noted was essential for "calculation." It is this that measures the worth of the outcomes that are being traded off. A second concept is needed too. In a trade-off, the pluses and minuses – the worths to us of the outcomes in view – are measured against each other, but only after some weights are attached, these being how likely or probable (possible) the different outcomes are. So the concept of a trade-off calls for a suitable concept of probability.

The Greeks had no such concept. They spoke of something that is translated as "the probable," by which they seem to have meant whatever squared with experience or with the facts, whatever could be part of a believable but less than certain report or prediction. Thus Aristotle again: "a probability is that which happens usually but not always. . . . "[12] Their concept allowed for comparisons: "One [proposition] may indeed be more likely to be true than the other. . . . "[13] But its uses were narrowly limited. The probable did not come in degrees, what was known was not held to be probable, and there were no low probabilities; what was *un*usual was not probable at all. The probability that a proposition had did not mark anyone's confidence in it, or how much confidence the hypothesis deserved (in itself, not compared to others). A trade-off of harms against benefits, of *risks* of harms against *promise* of benefits, could not therefore be conceived, and the theory of practical reason couldn't take trade-offs into account.

One might ask why the Greeks never worked out anything like our quantitative concept. No doubt it had something to do with their common disdain of "opinion." Plato dismissed the whole subject: "probability [is] that which the many think."[14] Also, to understand probabilities, it helps to focus on chance,

12 Aristotle, *Rhetoric,* 1402b.
13 Aristotle, *On Interpretation,* 19a.   14 *Phaedrus,* 273.

and that, for the Greeks, meant the unforeseeable. They spoke of knowledge as a body of truths shown to follow from principles. Since what was chancy couldn't be known, it wasn't deserving of study. Indeed, to think too much about chance reflected some cowardice and a lack of character; at least, that seems to have been the special Athenian view of the matter.[15] In life itself, nothing was certain – this was admitted by all. But that made for epic and drama, not for proper knowledge. Perhaps their geometric arithmetic and their awkward notation for numbers had some bearing here too.

However the fact is accounted for, the Greeks had no grasp of the sort of probabilities that figure in trade-off thinking. So, again, they couldn't think about trade-offs. In practice, this may not have made much difference. They did what seemed to them best "on the whole," accepting certain trade-offs and rejecting others. They couldn't reflect on their doing it, but people often do very well what they cannot reflect upon. Still, their theory fell short of their practice. They had no full theory of practical reasoning, if by that we mean (as above) a theory of the thinking that leads to action. Where a person starts with uncertainty, he has to work out his course from there. This working-out is part of his thinking. It ought to be covered by any theory of how he acts.

2.3 CHANCES AND ODDS

You are in a sordid gambling den (never mind now how you got there) and are being invited to play. Should you accept the odds that are offered? How much ought you to stake? This has to do with the chances of winning and how you ought to respond to them. As a modern amateur gamester, you can handle these questions, and in that you are better off than most of the wise

15 See Lowell Edmunds, *Chance and Intelligence in Thucydides* (Cambridge, Mass.: Harvard University Press, 1975), Chap. 2.

men who ever lived. How were you brought to this? A very quick run-through is all we will need.

We will begin in the Middle Ages. The Church then banned all forms of gambling. It went full out against gambling with dice, against which, however, it had little effect. The dice had too strong an appeal, for which we can now be glad. For it was the lure of dicing that led to the logic of chance.

The first big step in that direction was taken in a manuscript of about the year 960. The author of this, Bishop Wibold of Cambrai, grasped the basic theoretical point. He saw that different numbers of dice provide for different numbers of combinations. This prompted him to study the number of the possible outcomes of tossing several dice – the number of outcomes irrespective of order. (Wibold was not a gambler himself; he wanted to save people's souls. He assigned a special virtue to each of the 56 ways that three dice could fall and directed his monks to practice the virtue their throw had selected for them.)

Several centuries seem to have passed before the different orders of falls that yield the same combinations were distinguished. At least, there is no record of this before the thirteenth century. An enumeration of the possible outcomes of a three-dice throw counting differences in order appears at that time in the poem *De Vetula*, which is thought by some historians to have been written by Richard de Fournival. Whoever wrote it was ahead of his time. The author makes use of binomial coefficients in his computation of the number of possibilities, and this may be the first occasion of their being put to this use, the first by about four hundred years.

I should say that this sort of counting of combinations wasn't really new. The later Greeks had engaged in such studies, asking how many different syllables could be formed of the letters of the alphabet and how many molecular compounds could be formed of a given set of atomic propositions. The use of binomial coefficients was familiar to the Arabs and, before them, to the Chinese. And there was also a long tradition of combinatorial analysis among the Jews.[16] What is novel in the Middle Ages is only the application of such thinking to dicing, though indeed its having reached the Christian West was itself important. The *De Vetula* treatment of combinations is a milestone of doubtful significance. Still, it marks the achievement of an essential sophistication. It reveals a grasp of the fact that most combinations of dice falls can be variously realized.

The next step was to note the greater likelihood of the occurrence of those combinations that might be realized in more ways – those that are compatible with a larger number of orderings of the items involved. This important step was taken by the end of the fifteenth century. An author of the period says, "Concerning these throws it is to be observed that the dice are square and every face turns up, so that a number [a sum of dice faces] that can appear in more ways must appear more frequently. . . . "[17] Likewise for the set of the numbers on the different dice faces. Only a single question remained. Granted that a set of numbers that can appear in more ways will do so more often, how much more often should we expect it? To answer this, one step more was needed. There is a finite number of ways in which any set of numbers might appear. Each of the basic possibilities had to be said to be equally likely.

An issue might have been raised at this point. Which are the basic possibilities? Today we speak of *partitions* and *permutations*. Where three dice are being tossed, three sixes is one parti-

---

16 Combinatorial thinking among the Greeks is discussed in S. Sambursky, "On the Possible and the Probable in Ancient Greece," *Osiris* 12 (1956). The Jewish literature is surveyed in Nachum L. Rabinovitch, *Probability and Statistical Inference in Ancient and Medieval Jewish Literature* (Toronto: University of Toronto Press, 1973). F. N. David remarks on the history of binomial coefficients in her *Games, Gods and Gambling* (New York: Hafner, 1962), p. 34.

17 Quoted in M. G. Kendall, "The Beginnings of a Probability Calculus," *Biometrika* 43 (1956); reprinted in E. S. Pearson and M. G. Kendall (eds.), *Studies in the History of Statistics and Probability* (Darien: Hafner, 1970). In this and the preceding two paragraphs, I am drawing heavily on Kendall.

tion, two sixes and a four is another. But three sixes can be tossed in only one way: 6,6,6. Two sixes and a four can be tossed in three ways: 6,6,4, 6,4,6, and 4,6,6. We say that there is only one permutation of the three-sixes partition but three permutations of the two-sixes-and-a-four partition. Wibold was counting partitions; Fournival was counting permutations. Which are the basic possibilities, the 56 partitions or the 216 permutations? Should each partition or each permutation be assigned the same likelihood?

Philosophers have struggled with this. They have sometimes come down for partitions, which puts things in the more abstract way. To say that a toss is a two-sixes-and-a-four is to describe it more abstractly or loosely than to say it is a 6,4,6 (in that specific order). Leibniz may have taken partitions to be basic, and, in our own century, Carnap did. These writers held that, since we are thinking *a priori*, the more abstract the basis, the better. The earlier theorists didn't see it that way. They took the line now generally taken: the basic possibilities are permutations. The first explicit setting of equal likelihoods on permutations and the first derivation of other likelihoods from that initial setting are in a book by Cardano. (The book was written in 1563 or 1564 but was not published until 1663.)

Cardano considers this question, what is the chance or *probability* (though this word did not come till later) that the sum of the faces of two dice tossed together is some number n? He counts the ways of getting each possible sum, the different permutations favorable to each. He then finds the chance of getting n in the ratio of the number of n-favoring permutations to the total number of permutations. He also studies the chance of getting a 1 or a 2 or a 3 at least once when two dice are tossed, this by the same method of counting favorable permutations and forming the ratio to the total number.

He then turns to the chances of such outcomes where three dice are tossed, counts things wrong and gets confused, but works it out correctly in the end, or so his biographer Oystein

Ore argues in his plausible analysis of the book.[18] Ore takes the book to be a kind of journal of the author's thoughts on the subject, the initial errors being there along with the later and sounder results. What is clear is that Cardano was still groping. The questions he was studying were still difficult problems.

No longer so two generations later, when Galileo was consulted about them. Galileo wrote a brief note on this question that had been put to him: how does it happen that though the number of partitions favorable to getting a sum of 9 with three dice is the same as the number of partitions that are favorable to getting a 10 (there are six in each case), a sum of 10 appears more often than a sum of 9? Count the permutations, says Galileo. There are 27 permutations favorable to a sum of 10 and only 25 favorable to a sum of 9, so the chance of the former is greater than that of the latter. Galileo's discussion is confident and clear. The greater frequency of 10 has "a very obvious reason," he says. Though in the early seventeenth century these matters could still be puzzling (else why consult Galileo about them?), they were no longer difficult. At least there were those who could handle them.[19]

By the time of Galileo, one could make proper judgments of odds. So we have finally come to an answer to one of our gambling-den questions, if only a partial, negative answer. The question was whether the gambler should play the game he is being invited to play. He *oughtn't* to play unless the odds on his winning reflect the chances or probabilities. The principle appears in Cardano's book:

> . . . there is a general rule, namely, that we should consider the whole circuit [the number of all the permutations], and the number of those casts which represent in how many ways the favorable result can occur, and compare that number to the

18 Oystein Ore, *Cardano; the Gambling Scholar* (Princeton: Princeton University Press, 1953). Cardano's book is printed as an appendix to Ore's biography of him.
19 Galileo's note appears as Appendix 2 in David, *Games, Gods and Gambling*.

remainder of the circuit, and according to that proportion should the mutual wagers be laid so that one may contend on equal terms.[20]

Again, this rests on a way now developed of thinking about chances or probabilities: the probability of an event is the number of permutations favorable to its occurrence divided by the number of all the permutations possible. This was not made fully explicit until some hundred years after Galileo, but we can already find it present in the reasoning of these earlier thinkers.

That is, we find either this idea or some other like it. For a second idea too would accord with Galileo's discussion. We might hold that the probabilities he noted weren't any ratios of possible outcomes, that the ratios were only the indices of these probabilities. A probability itself, on this second construal, is the credibility of an outcome for the agent, the degree of belief he is entitled to assign to, say, a sum of 9 with three dice. Or we might take still a third line on this and hold that the probability that Galileo established was his actual degree of belief in the dice showing a sum of 9, a degree of belief to which it happens he was entitled by the nature of the case, by the ratio of the relevant permutations.

The theory of people's reasons must reach beyond their beliefs and desires – that is the thesis to be argued in this book. We need a broader psychological framework, and we will shortly get to the project of taking in understandings. With that same larger purpose in view, we will now let probabilities be the degrees of belief people have, their actual, current degrees of belief. I don't suggest that the early thinkers meant just this by probability. Very likely, they didn't mean this, but that need not trouble us here. Their thinking accorded with the idea of probabilities as degrees of belief, though it accorded equally with the credibility and the ratio-of-possibilities ideas.[21]

20 Cardano, *De Ludo Aleae*, in Ore, *Cardano*, p. 202.
21 The question of what they may have meant is taken up by Ian Hacking in his *The Emergence of Probability* (Cambridge University Press, 1975).

2.4 EXPECTEDNESS

It isn't always clear what all the permutations are. A die has six faces, so where n dice are tossed, there are 6^n permutations. (Cardano first stated this power law.) But sometimes, unlike with dice faces, the atoms involved don't announce themselves. It then isn't obvious how many there are, and so the number of permutations isn't obvious either. In such a case, many problems remain.

One such residual issue in this period was the so-called division problem, also known as the problem of points. This can be traced to the fourteenth century, but it is likely to be much older, and possibly of Arabic origin. Two people here play a game in stages, each stage being worth one point, the players having an equal chance of winning each of the points. The first to win a certain number of points will get a certain amount of money. The game is cut short before either player has all the points he needs, and it is decided to divide the money. How ought it to be divided if what may be considered is only how many points each player has? Many of the thinkers of the early period struggled with a problem of this sort, but none of them found a correct solution.[22]

The early period closed with a famous exchange of letters between Pascal and Fermat. We have in this correspondence (in 1654) the first proper treatment of a division problem – indeed, we have *two* proper treatments. Also, and more important, we find here a lucid application of a new principle of practical reason. The idea itself was not new at all, but it had never been made explicit. The thinking expressed in this set of letters prompted others to do just that.[23]

Pascal wrote to Fermat because he wanted to confirm his solution of some problems that had been put to him. One of

22 See Kendall, "The Beginnings of a Probability Calculus," for a history of the problem. See also Oystein Ore, "Pascal and the Invention of Probability Theory," *American Mathematical Monthly* 67 (1960).

23 The letters are printed as Appendix 4 in David, *Games, Gods, and Gambling*.

these was a division problem. Three points are needed to win. The game had been stopped when one player had one point and the other player had none. The prize is 64 pistoles. How ought it to be divided? Pascal argues this way: suppose that Jacques had *two* points and that Pierre had *one* – call this situation *A*. If Jacques won the next point, he would get the whole 64; if he lost, the score would be tied, and so he would be entitled to 32. Since he could be sure of 32 and would have an even chance of getting 32 more, he would here be entitled to 32 + 16.

Consider next the case in which Jacques has two points and Pierre has none – call this situation *B*. If Jacques won the next point, he would get 64; if he lost, he would be in *A*, where he is entitled to 48. He can count on 48 and has an even chance of getting 16 more, so he is entitled to 48 + 8. Finally, take the situation of the initial problem. Jacques here has one point and Pierre has none. If Jacques won the next point, he would be in *B*, where he is entitled to 56; if he lost, the score would be tied, which would entitle him to 32. So he can be sure of 32 and has an even chance of getting 24 more, which entitles him to 32 + 12. It follows that Jacques should get 44 and Pierre the other 20.

Fermat worked out a simple combinatorial analysis. He noted that the game, if continued, would last at most four more steps. Each step would yield a point either to Jacques or to Pierre. There are 16 permutations of Jacques-points and Pierre-points in four steps of the game, and each of these is equally likely. When we write them all down, we see that 11 would make the winner Jacques and 5 would declare for Pierre. So the prize of 64 pistoles should be divided in that proportion, that is, Jacques should get 44 and Pierre should get 20. Fermat's result is the same as Pascal's, and we accept this result today.

I say that Fermat's analysis is simple. It wasn't thought simple in his own time. Pascal himself thought the labor "excessive." Still, the counting of permutations was not in any way new. If it wasn't always thought simple, it was at least a familiar idea.

28

Pascal's recursive method of analysis was not a total novelty either. Over a century earlier, Giovanni Peverone had studied a division problem in a similar manner. But Peverone made an error and did not get the proper answer, and it is unlikely that Pascal knew his work.[24] So the credit for coming in first clearly belongs to Pascal. Besides, it isn't the recursion itself that calls for attention here. It is the logic at each separate stage.

Again, Jacques had one point and Pierre had none. To how much of the 64-pistole prize is Jacques now entitled? Let us take the question to be what playing the game was worth to him at the stage it had reached. What would be fair compensation to him for the game's having been stopped? Pascal answers this way, that since Jacques had an even chance of moving to a situation that was worth 56 to him or to one that was worth 32, going on with the game was worth $(\frac{1}{2} \times 56) + (\frac{1}{2} \times 32)$ to him, and that is therefore his due. (The values of the two hypothetical situations – 56 and 32 – are found the same way.)

To us today, this thinking is clear. It determines the value of an option by studying the possible gains that it offers. The project is to find the average of the values of its possible outcomes, the *weighted* average of them, the weights being the probabilities of these outcomes, or (often better) of the different contingencies in which they would be met. In Pascal's time, this averaging method was not yet the obvious course it is now, though it was implicit in every gambler's evaluation of the bets that he made.

Some of the bets then were intricate. Consider the bet that would yield you 60 pistoles if in 24 tosses of two dice a double six occurred at least once. How much should you be willing to pay for the option of placing this bet? (Pascal was consulted on this very question.) The tricky part is to find the probability of winning; that probability is .4914.[25] The rest is easy: the probability of losing is $1 - .4914$, or .5086, and the value of the bet is

---

24 For Peverone, see Kendall, "The Beginnings of a Probability Calculus."
25 It is $1 - (^{35}/_{36})^{24}$, which equals .4914.

thus $(.4914 \times 60) + (.5086 \times 0)$, or 29.484 pistoles. Here too we have weighted averaging. But since in such cases a loss yields nothing and the second summand drops out, there is no need to attend to all of the averaging logic of the calculation. The virtue of Pascal's treatment of his division problem was that it called attention to it.

Pascal did not present the logic in any formal way. This was first done by Huygens, who was in Paris shortly after the famous correspondence. He had met neither Pascal nor Fermat, nor did he see the letters, but he must have heard about the nature of the discussions in them. Back home again in Holland, he wrote a short book on the principle involved, on what he called the principle of *expectation*.

Here is his initial statement: "I shall make use of this principle, one's hazard or expectation to gain any thing is worth so much as, if he had it, he could purchase the like hazard or expectation again in a just and equal game."[26] The "worth" or value of a game is what (in fairness) one could be charged to play it, the most a sensible person would pay. Huygens shows that, on this principle, the value of a game is the probability-weighted average of the values of its possible outcomes. Following Huygens, we call this today the *expected value* or *expectedness* of the game. We now speak likewise of the expected value of an option *in* a game. The expected value for Jacques of the option of continuing his game is 44 pistoles, and Huygens indeed uses Pascal's analysis to illustrate the new principle.

Though Huygens speaks only of games, we can move beyond them and speak of the expected value of any option whatever. All this requires is that the agent thinks it might have different outcomes, that he isn't certain of what the outcome would be. Take, for instance, a doctor considering whether to prescribe a

26 This is taken from John Arbuthnot's printing of Huygens' book in his *Of the Laws of Chance, or, a Method of Calculation of the Hazards of Game* (London, 1714), p. 2.

new drug. If the drug did not trigger an allergy, it would cure his patient, but if it did it would kill him – or so the doctor believes. Suppose that he sets specific values on these two possible outcomes (what this means we will come to shortly) and also sets some probability on the drug's being safe. The treatment he is considering then has an expected value. If this is greater than that of any alternative, he makes up his mind to prescribe the drug.

What we have here is twofold. First, we have the idea that the expected values measure the worth of every option. Second, we have a thesis about how a person moves out of uncertainty. Which of his options will a person trying to make up his mind come to want – how will such a person choose? The thesis is that he will choose the option that has the greatest expected value, or any one of them, if there are several. We will find it convenient to refer to both these ideas as the principle of expectedness.

A marginal note about the doctor's thinking. The doctor has some degree of belief that the drug is safe. How does he establish this probability? Clearly he does not establish it the way the gambler works out the odds; the counting and comparing of permutations makes no sense in his case. The doctor goes by the record of successful treatments with the drug he might use. This raises no problem for us. Recall that probabilities do not depend on ratios of numbers of possibilities. The concept of possibility ratios got people to develop the theory of this subject. It led them to study the logic of probability, to grasp the idea of *coherent* probabilities (the topic of Section 2.8). But probabilities, as we here construe them, are degrees of belief, and these were there from the start. They were there before any gamblers came to think about odds.

2.5 A PARADOX

One more idea must be brought in, and for that we must skip almost a century. Strictly, it is only for its first announcement

that we must reach ahead. The idea itself was not foreign to
Pascal and to Huygens and to the others of their time, but they
found no need to remark in any way on it. An unlikely little
problem finally put it on the map.

The idea was that of utility, and the problem was the St.
Petersburg problem, first reported in print by Daniel Bernoulli in
1738.[27] Bernoulli did not claim that there was anything original
in his idea: "a person who is fairly judicious by natural instinct
might have realized and spontaneously applied [it]. . . . "[28] He
took credit only for his special psychological analysis of it.

The idea is this, that in thinking about expectedness, "the
determination of the *value* of an event must not be based on its
price, but rather on the *utility* it yields. The price of an item is
dependent only on the thing itself and is equal for everyone; the
utility, however, is dependent on the particular circumstances of
the person making the estimate."[29] Bernoulli goes on to illustrate. A gain of a certain amount of money means more to a
poor man than to a rich one, though a small sum will matter
much to a millionaire if he needs it for something essential
(perhaps to complete a ransom). He notes that what led him to
study these matters was the following problem by his cousin
Nicholas Bernoulli:

> Peter tosses a coin and continues to do so until it should land
> "heads" when it comes to the ground. He agrees to give Paul
> one ducat if he gets "heads" on the very first throw, two duc-
> ats if he gets it on the second, four if on the third, eight if on
> the fourth, and so on, so that with each additional throw the
> number of ducats he must pay is doubled. Suppose we seek to
> determine the value of Paul's expectation.[30]

27 In a contribution to the *Proceedings of the St. Petersburg Academy of Sciences* –
hence the name "St. Petersburg problem." A translation appears in *Econometrica* 22 (1954); this is reprinted in Alfred N. Page (ed.), *Utility Theory: A
Book of Readings* (New York: Wiley, 1968).
28 In Page, *Utility Theory*, p. 208.   29 Ibid., p. 201.   30 Ibid., p. 209.

A Paradox

The problem is to find the expected value of being the Paul-side of this game. How much should someone be willing to pay to step into Paul's shoes? An expectation (expectedness) is a probability-weighted average of the values of the possible outcomes. So the expectation here is the ducat to be got if the first toss is heads times the probability of a head on the first toss, *plus* the two ducats to be got if the first head is on the second toss times the probability of *that* outcome, *plus*.... That is, it is $(1 \times \frac{1}{2}) + (2 \times \frac{1}{4}) + (4 \times \frac{1}{8}) + \ldots$, which is $\frac{1}{2} + \frac{1}{2} + \frac{1}{2} + \ldots$. On this analysis, the expectation is infinite, and we now have a paradox. For no one would pay an infinite sum to take Paul's place in this game, nor would Paul demand such a sum. Bernoulli says that a "reasonable" Paul would be happy to sell for twenty ducats but would almost certainly not find any takers.

Bernoulli suggests that the problem derives from putting expectations in terms of money. Let them instead be the probability-weighted averages of the *utilities* of the possible outcomes. The outcomes here are still sums of money. But consider now that money has a decreasing marginal utility, that every increment of any amount of money matters less to the person who gets it than did the preceding increment of that size. If this is true of Paul, the expected value of the game for him is not $\frac{1}{2} + \frac{1}{2} + \frac{1}{2} + \ldots$ but a sum of decreasing fractions that asymptotically approaches some finite number. (The probabilities of the outcomes still diminish geometrically, but their utilities are no longer geometrically increasing.) Bernoulli goes a step further and proposes a theory of the utility of money that yields expected values that are not only finite but low. The value of the game for any particular person turns out to be just what that person would pay, and this retires the paradox.

Bernoulli's analysis does not do the job, for we can bring the paradox back. Let Peter change his offer. How much money he will pay now reflects the utilities Paul sets. If the first toss is heads, Paul will get the amount of money on which he sets a utility of 1 (however this value is set). If the first head comes on the second toss, he will get whatever amount of money has a utility of 2 for him; if the first head comes on the third toss, he will get the amount of money to which he assigns a utility of 4, etc. On the utility construal of expectedness, the value of this second game is infinite, and so we have a paradox again, for no one is likely to pay very much to buy out Paul in this game either.

This is Karl Menger's response to Bernoulli. Menger offers a different analysis, but that analysis doesn't work either. He holds that what the paradox tells us is that utilities must always be bounded, that there must be some finite number n than which no utility of Paul's is greater.[31] But what would follow in that case is only that the value of the game would be finite. The value of the game might be n, the upper bound of Paul's utilities — it *would* be n for certain series of money outcomes — and that is still much too large.

Other solutions have been suggested. One of these is Fontaine's.[32] This notes that the game that Peter proposes is not the same as the one he would play, for he cannot live up to his promise in every situation in which he might be. If the first head came on the twenty-third toss, he would owe Paul over four million dollars (enough about ducats!), and that is more money than he has. In fact, it is likely he would run out much sooner. Suppose he has only 10,000 dollars and that the first head comes on the fifteenth toss. If Peter gave as much as he could, Paul would get not the 16,384 due him but only 10,000 — that is all Peter has. So Peter has been misleading Paul. If he has only 10,000, the expected value of the game is not infinite but only

---

31 Karl Menger, "Das Unsicherheitsmoment in der Wertlehre," *Zeitschrift für Nationalökonomie* 5 (1934). A translation appears in Martin Shubik (ed.), *Essays in Mathematical Economics in Honor of Oskar Morgenstern* (Princeton: Princeton University Press, 1967).

32 I take the citation from Isaac Todhunter's *A History of the Mathematical Theory of Probability* (New York: Chelsea, 1965), p. 261.

$7 + (\underline{10,000} \times {}^{1}/_{32,768}) + (\underline{10,000} \times {}^{1}/_{65,536}) + (\underline{10,000} \times {}^{1}/_{131,072}) + \ldots$, which comes to just over $7^{1}/_{2}$. This puts it in dollar values; put in utilities, the worth of the game is the value Paul sets on whatever he would pay just over $7.50 to get. No doubt that is better than making its price infinite (or putting the price at the upper utility bound), but it remains a larger sum than many people would pay.[33]

A fourth solution is that of D'Alembert, who held that whatever is very improbable ought to be seen as impossible and ignored.[34] D'Alembert rests this unlikely thesis on a distinction of two kinds of possibility, physical and metaphysical. His example is that of getting two sixes with two dice 100 times in a row; he holds this to be metaphysically possible but says that it isn't *physically* possible, for it never happened and never will. This is a very unpromising distinction.

Still, there is a second distinction that he may have intended. Let us say that a metaphysical possibility is one not excluded by logic alone and that a physical (better, *doxastic*) possibility is one not excluded by what the agent believes. The next ten tosses all being tails is metaphysically (or logically) possible, but, *for me*, it isn't physically possible, since I believe that this will not happen. Sufficiently low probabilities often lead a person into disbelief. Thus an event of low probability (100 double sixes or even ten tails) may, for the agent, not be physically possible. If he goes by physical possibility, by what he believes, he is then right to ignore it.

Or we might distinguish directly among probabilities instead. We can speak of probabilities that are independent of what the

---

33 This was noted by D'Alembert; see Todhunter, ibid. p. 261. Still, in the next century, Poisson returned to the limited-funds idea; see George J. Stigler, "The Development of Utility Theory," *Journal of Political Economy* 86 (1950), reprinted in Page, *Utility Theory*, p. 87. It is revived in Richard C. Jeffrey, *The Logic of Decision*, 2d ed. (Chicago: University of Chicago Press, 1983), pp. 154–5.

34 Again, see Todhunter, *A History of the Mathematical Theory of Probability*, p. 262. See also Paul A. Samuelson, "St. Petersburg Paradoxes: Defanged, Dissected, and Historically Described," *Journal of Economic Literature* 15 (1977).

agent believes and of probabilities relative to his beliefs, of probabilities *a priori* and *a posteriori*. The ten-tails sequence has an *a priori* probability of $1/1{,}024$, but, for Paul (who believes it won't happen), it has an *a posteriori* probability of 0. The expectedness principle is clearly meant to be read in terms of posterior probabilities. Thus if Paul believes that at least one head will appear in the first ten tosses (and admits every other heads-and-tails combination), the expected value of the game for him is $(1 \times 512/1{,}023) + (2 \times 256/1{,}023) + (4 \times 128/1{,}023) + \ldots + (512 \times 1/1{,}023) + (1{,}024 \times 0) + (2{,}048 \times 0) + (4{,}096 \times 0) + \ldots$, which comes to just over 5. If he believes that a head will appear in the first *eight* tosses, the game is worth just over 4, etc.

The basic idea is that where the prior probability of a certain outcome is low, the agent then sometimes believes it won't happen. He not only doubts that it will; he believes that it won't. The low probability of that outcome leads to disbelief, and the disbelief makes the *posterior* probability zero. (The low prior probability of ten tails in a row leads Paul to believe that there won't be ten tails, which makes for a zero posterior probability for that outcome.) If we accept this analysis and put expectedness in terms of posterior probabilities, we can explain why many (most) people would pay very little to take Paul's place. Certain of his prospects are too improbable for them: their thresholds of disbelief are soon crossed. Also why some would pay more than others: thresholds of disbelief vary.[35]

But is there always a threshold? If so, we have a new problem. Let your threshold of disbelief be the probability $1/t$ – make it as low as you like – and imagine a fair lottery with more than

35 Buffon suggested the probability of a 56-year-old man dying within the day as a furthest threshold of disbelief – anything more unlikely ought to be disbelieved; see Stigler, "The Development of Utility Theory," p. 87. Emile Borel developed the thresholds idea into a general principle of reason; see his *Probabilities and Life* (New York: Dover, 1962). The idea is proposed anew in Samuel Gorovitz, "The St. Petersburg Puzzle," in Maurice Allais and Ole Hagen (eds.), *Expected Utility Hypotheses and the Allais Paradox* (Dordrecht: Reidel, 1979).

t tickets. The probability that ticket 1 will win is less than $1/t$. Its winning is too improbable, so you believe that it won't. Likewise for every other ticket, so you believe that no ticket will win. But that goes flat against your belief that the lottery is fair: that some ticket will be drawn.[36]

Should we say that there sometimes are thresholds and sometimes (perhaps in lotteries) not? Or should we say that our thresholds can change, that we adjust them to avoid this sort of trouble? Or are our thresholds not for disbelief but for doubt, for *non*belief only (this would leave Paul in the lurch)? I will pass these questions by.

2.6 UTILITIES

Two points emerge about the St. Petersburg problem. The first is that Bernoulli's discussion doesn't dispose of the paradox – recall the Menger restatement of that. The second is that this need not detain us, that the problem can be handled, though another (the lottery problem) then requires attention. The issue and Bernoulli's analysis of it remain important because they made utilities central. The nature of utilities now became a serious question on its own.

Bernoulli wrote of the utility that a certain sum of money "yields." This makes for an ambiguity. The utility yielded might be some property or quality of the money itself, perhaps a contingent property, one that depends on the circumstances, the utility of any amount of money depending on how much you already have. The money "yields" utility here in the way that trees yield lumber. Or the utility might be something separate from the money but related to it – for instance, the pleasure that spending it offers or the need or desire you have for it. The same,

36 The lottery problem was first presented by Henry E. Kyburg; see his *Probability and the Logic of Rational Belief* (Middletown: Wesleyan University Press, 1961), p. 197.

of course, where we go beyond money: the utility of any item might be either *intrinsic* or *extrinsic* to it.

Until the twentieth century, the concept was mainly of the former sort; that is, the principal writers mostly thought of utility as being intrinsic. Bentham put it this way: "By utility is meant that property in any object whereby it tends to produce benefit, advantage, pleasure, good, or happiness."[37] This made the utility of an object one of its basic properties and took the benefit or pleasure it yields to be something else. Likewise, Jevons defined utility as "the abstract quality whereby an object serves our purposes,"[38] these purposes being the having of pleasure and the avoidance of pain. Still, this makes for too neat a divide. Claiming to speak for "every writer, from Epicurus to Bentham, who maintained the theory of utility," J. S. Mill brought in the other concept and said that utility was "pleasure itself, together with exemption from pain."[39] It is likely that the two concepts often were not distinguished.

We need to distinguish them here. When we spoke of the different ways of conceiving of probability, we reminded ourselves of our project of expanding the theory of belief-and-desire reasons. If our theory is to be general, it must apply where the agent is uncertain. So we decided to take probabilities to be the degrees of belief people have, for these can be said to reflect a kind of uncertainty, a doxastic or beliefwise uncertainty. The theory also has to allow for a lack of certainty of desire, and this now suggests that we adopt the second of our two concepts of utility. On that, the utility of an item isn't something in it that makes it useful or pleasant but rather the degree of use that the

---

37 Jeremy Bentham, *An Introduction to the Principles of Morals and Legislation*, in Edwin A. Burtt (ed.), *The English Philosophers from Bacon to Mill* (New York: Random House, 1939), p. 792.
38 William Stanley Jevons, *The Theory of Political Economy* (Harmondsworth: Penguin, 1970), p. 101.
39 John Stuart Mill, *Utilitarianism*, in Burtt, *The English Philosophers from Bacon to Mill*, p. 899.

agent has for this item. Or better (setting *use* aside), it is his degree of *desire* for it, for getting it or for keeping it.

The neglect of the distinction of the concepts of utility has been a source of much needless trouble. It has led some critics to dismiss utility theory as being simplistic. The theory endorses the commensurability of every good (and bad), and this, these critics insist, is a myth. They deny that there is any property common to every good (and bad) the quantity of which determines how much of a good (or bad) it is. There is no common ingredient of a good day's work and a good night's sleep – and of a friend, a skill, a raise, a poem, etc.

All this is true but not worrisome. It carries some weight against Bentham and Jevons but not against our concept of utilities as a person's degrees of desire. Degrees of desire are commensurable. Either a person wants x more than y, or he wants y more than x, or he ranks them on a par, whatever x and y may be. This too of course might be challenged, but I think it will stand (with a gloss to be added shortly). If we depart from Bentham and Jevons, we can thus have it both ways. We can deny the existence of any common value-ingredient of goods and hold nonetheless that all goods are comparable in terms of the comparer's degree of desire for them.

Describing utilities as degrees of desire says very little about what they are. It says that utilities are states of the agent, but it gives no particulars. It doesn't say they are feeling states or neurological matters or dispositions to act. Likewise where we describe probabilities as the agent's degrees of belief, for nothing has been said as yet about what a degree of belief might be. We can't take the degree-phrases literally. Belief and desire don't come in degrees; you either believe or want x or you don't. How then ought we to take them? Besides, one might ask, what is belief itself, and also, what is desire – what is the *wanting* of something? I can offer no definitions of beliefs or desires; that is, I have no definitions of the usual reductivist sort. Nor have I any such definitions of utilities or probabilities.

So the question remains to be faced: what are we talking about? Granted that utilities and probabilities and the rest are states of the agent and not of the world around him, what is true of these states he is in that is not also true of others? On any theory, what is true of just them is what that theory says about them. And what our present theory says attributes a certain role to them.

The theory says that people act on their reasons and that their reasons are composed of beliefs and desires. We can't define these states separately, but the theory pins them down as a pair: beliefs and desires are mental states that sometimes, when they mesh, make for action. The theory also says that a person comes to want what on the whole seems best, or any of his best-seeming options. Also that what seems best on the whole is what has the greatest expectedness. A person's utilities and probabilities together establish expectedness for him, and so they determine what he will want. Thus these states are pinned down too: a person's utilities and probabilities are states of which this last thesis is true.

Time now to pull all these threads together. We noted at the start that the Aristotelian idea takes no account of uncertainty. The ancients said nothing about how people *choose*, how a person makes up his mind, how he comes to want this or that. The theory of choosing took a while to develop. It appears now in the principle of expectedness – the principle of expected utility. So the larger idea is this. Suppose that a person has several options, none of which he initially wants: he is desire-uncertain about them. Suppose that he wants to make up his mind. He chooses the option (or one of the options) that has the greatest expected utility. The rest is the Aristotelian thesis. Let what the agent chose be x. If he believes that x requires (or presupposes or is in part realized by) y and that he might now bring about y, he now brings it about – if he is driven and unimpeded.

In situations without uncertainty, this reduces to just the last bit. All we need here is that if someone wants x and believes that

x requires (or presupposes . . .) y and that he might now bring about y, he now brings it about. In special cases, it boils down even further. Here too the agent isn't uncertain; say he wants x from the start. He thinks he could bring about x directly (no need to do anything else). In cases like this, y merges with x. The agent wants x, which he knows requires x, and he thinks he can bring x about. So he goes right to it. (Call his reason here *vacuous*, for his belief about what x requires is vacuous; in a *non*-vacuous reason, x is distinct from y.)

The introduction of expected utilities does not affect our concept of a reason. A person's reasons for what he does remain some beliefs and desires he has, and an explanation in terms of reasons needs to refer just to these. Still, where we ask about those reasons – where we want to know why he has them – we have to take in more. If the agent started uncertain, we want to see how he settled his mind, and here his expected utilities enter. (They enter where he was *conatively* uncertain and moved from there to some full desire; we have said nothing about how he moves from *doxastic* uncertainty to belief.)

But how do his expected utilities explain why the agent wants what he does? An explanandum must follow from its explanans, and it doesn't follow just from the expected utilities being what they are that the agent wants x. We have to add an assumption here about what moves this person, an assumption like that of drivenness in Section 2.1. We have to say that he is being *rational*, this in the sense that he wants what has the greatest expected utility (and wants it because of this). From x's having the greatest expected utility *plus* the agent's now being rational it does indeed follow that he wants x.

We asked above, when we added drivenness, whether that made the theory tautologous. The question might be asked here too, and here again the answer is *no*. The assumption we are adding is that the agent is being rational, and that alone is no tautology. There can be evidence both for and against it in what he is like in other situations. An explanans in which it figures need not have any tautology in it. What is tautologous is only the statement that the explanandum follows from the explanans, and a statement of what follows from what has to be either tautologous or false.

The theory presented has recently come against criticism from several sides. Its basic ideas have been faulted and its judgments dismissed. We will briefly look at just a few of these challenges here. Let me say that, in my opinion, these first challenges all can be met. The theory holds up against them. (Others that are less tractable are taken up in Chapter 4.)

Some critiques I will set aside. In particular, I will say nothing about the most radical lines of attack. These reject our central concepts of belief and desire as much too crude, as concepts that can't be squared with a proper science of mind. Theories based on these old ideas are dismissed as "folk psychology." It is held that they must be replaced by theories whose terms have better credentials, terms reflecting the work being done in neurophysiology or in cognitive science.[40] I think this approach is as wrong as can be, but it has been forcefully argued and a discussion would take us afield. Fortunately, we can beg off; there have been good discussions by others.[41]

A challenge of a different sort faults our conception of reasons. According to the theory above, a person always acts as he does because of the beliefs and desires he has. So we have a causal claim here. The objection is that it may be true, but that

---

40 This critique appears in Paul M. Churchland, *Scientific Realism and the Plasticity of Mind* (Cambridge University Press, 1979), and in Stephen P. Stich, *From Folk Psychology to Cognitive Science* (Cambridge, Mass.: MIT Press, 1983).
41 See Terence Horgan and James Woodward, "Folk Psychology Is Here To Stay," *Philosophical Review* 94 (1985); Jerry A. Fodor, *Psychosemantics* (Cambridge, Mass.: MIT Press, 1987); and William G. Lycan, *Judgment and Justification* (Cambridge University Press, 1988). See also Frank Jackson and Philip Pettit, "In Defence of Folk Psychology," *Philosophical Studies*, in press.

it isn't enough. The agent's causative belief-plus-desire needn't explain the action he took. In which case, why call it his reason? Donald Davidson puts it in terms of the action's not being intentional. He cites this example of Daniel Bennett's. Jones wants to be rid of Smith, his enemy. He thinks that this means he must kill him and also that he now has a chance. He fires and misses, but startles a herd of wild pigs who stampede and trample Smith, who dies. Smith is dead because Jones fired. But was the killing *intentional?* Can we say that his belief and desire explain Jones killing Smith? Were they the reason he did it?

Davidson offers a second example. Jones, a climber, is holding Smith on a rope. He wants to rid himself of the weight and danger and knows that this calls for loosening his grip. This desire-*cum*-belief so unnerves him that his grip in fact loosens. The rope slips out of his hand, and so he gets what he wanted: he is free of the weight. But did he do it intentionally? Can we explain his relaxing his grip in terms of the belief and desire he had?[42]

Davidson thinks that we can't, this because of the way in which the death of Smith came about. Smith died in both cases because of Jones, but Jones' beliefs and desires caused his death only indirectly. Intentional action implies a direct ("nondeviant") causation by a belief-and-desire pair. Davidson puts it like this: "The point is that not just any causal connection between rationalizing attitudes and a wanted effect suffices to guarantee that producing the wanted effect was intentional. The causal chain must follow the right sort of route."[43] The problem is to say what a right (or direct or nondeviant) causal route is.

I see these two cases differently. Take the shooting story. What keeps us from saying that Jones' belief and desire were his reason for killing Smith is not that he did it only indirectly (and therefore unintentionally) but that he didn't do it at all. He

---

42 Both examples are in Davidson's "Freedom to Act" in his *Essays on Actions and Events*, pp. 78, 79.

43 Ibid., p. 78.

didn't kill Smith; the pigs killed him. His firing brought it about that they did it, but he did not do it himself. So also in the climbing case. Jones did not relax his grip; the fact was just that his grip relaxed. It wasn't something that he did but something that happened to him. A "wanted effect" is a wanted action only if it is both wanted and an action, and the action condition here fails. (In the first story, the killing was an action, but on the pigs' part, not on Jones'.)

Thus far, we haven't found any problem. But what about that concept of action? When is a person not being an agent? When can't we say he is *doing* something? (What warrants the view that relaxing his grip wasn't something Jones *did?*) We can pass this question by. The question is on a level of thinking different from that of our theory. Economists study how people invest without first giving a definition of people, and we can speak of the reasons for actions without first defining action. This of course assumes agreement on the specifics in the cases before us, agreement on whether this or that was an action (Jones relaxing his grip). But there is in fact much agreement.

The moral of the Jones-Smith stories needn't give anyone pause. The moral is only that the effect of a reason isn't always some action. Davidson also presents a scenario that points to a different moral. Here he brings on Oedipus, a distant cousin of the famous Greek. This Oedipus is in a rush to kill his father. He finds an old man blocking his way. Eager to hasten his father's death, Oedipus kills this man; and in fact it was as he wanted, for the man was his father. He thought he was hastening his father's death and he wanted to do just that, and this belief and desire jointly caused him to do it. Davidson notes the devious way in which the fates here gratified Oedipus. This leads him to hold that "we could not say that in killing the old man he intentionally killed his father, nor that his reason in killing the old man was to kill his father."[44]

44 Davidson, "Psychology as Philosophy," *Essays on Actions and Events,* p. 232.

No question of this being an action. Oedipus did it, no doubt about that. Still, ought we to accept the conclusion that is drawn? That conclusion has two parts: "we could not say that . . . nor that. . . . " The first part is clearly correct; Oedipus didn't intentionally kill his father. He did intentionally kill the old man, and killing that man *was* killing his father, but this was just a physical sameness. We are here speaking of the intentionality of the action under a certain description, and that has to do with how the agent thinks the action might be described. A person does something intentionally under a given description of it only where he (correctly) believes that what he is doing can be so described. There was no intentional patricide, no intentional killing under a father-killing description, for Oedipus did not think when he did it that what he was doing was killing his father.

The first half of the conclusion is correct, but the second half doesn't follow: that Oedipus didn't intentionally kill his father has no bearing on the reason he had. A person's reason for what he is doing is what moves him to it. It is surely right to say that Oedipus was moved (in part) by his belief that to kill his father he had to kill the man then before him. So there is nothing wrong in saying that Oedipus' reason for killing the man was the belief (and desire) he had that it would let him get at his father. Nor is there anything wrong in saying that he *intended* to get at his father, that it was his *intention* to do this, if by his "intention" we mean his desire to do it. Doing it with this intention remains something different from doing it intention-ally, and that is the moral that might be drawn from Davidson's Oedipus myth.

The Jones-Smith and the Oedipus challenges are directed at the theory of belief-desire reasons, as is the folk-psychology critique. Critics have also faulted the sort of theory of uncertainty laid out above. They have held that actual thinking isn't as neat as that theory suggests. People don't always have precise degrees of belief and desire; at least they do not have them in the profusion that is required.[45] So they cannot always be said to set expected utilities on their options and can't be said always to maximize. Indeed, since degrees of belief and desire often are imprecise, the commensuration of utilities we posited a few pages ago breaks down, and that of probabilities does too. The imprecision of people's thinking threatens to undo our theory. In an earlier book I worked out a way of handling this problem. The course I suggested makes for complications we here do well to avoid; still, let me briefly describe it.

The idea is to let the usual analysis be just a special case, to generalize from precise degrees of belief and desire to *ranges* of them, from point-specific probabilities and utilities to *ranges* of probabilities and utilities. The extent of a person's refinement of judgment appears in the various ranges of these sorts – the narrower a range, the finer his judgment. Point-specific expected utilities give way to ranges of expected utilities, and the idea of maximizing can now be touched up too. (In my earlier book I show how.)[46]

About the commensuration of probabilities and utilities: a person's position on any matter may be specific or unspecific. Ranges may be only points or middling somehow or as wide as can be. So the commensuration of people's judgments is now a looser affair. It doesn't always (or even often) call for making pointwise comparisons. The comparisons need only be range-by-range, and the ranges may overlap. People's thinking is indeed messy, but it turns out we can live with that. Its being messy doesn't exclude an analysis of the sort we have here.

2.8 COHERENCE

We have yet to put expectedness in a properly general form. Bernoulli's concept had to do with simple sorts of situations

45 This is a common objection. See, for instance, Herbert A. Simon, *Models of Man* (New York: Wiley, 1957), Chap. 14.
46 See my *Having Reasons* (Princeton: Princeton University Press, 1984), Chaps. 2 and 3. A closely related treatment appears in Isaac Levi, *The Enterprise of Knowledge* (Cambridge, Mass.: MIT Press, 1980), Chap. 4.

only. The expected utility of an option is the weighted average of the utilities set on its possible outcomes, and in a Bernoulli situation, the weights are the probabilities of these outcomes. Better, the weights are the probabilities of the various contexts in which these outcomes would be met.

Suppose now that some game would yield us five dollars in a certain context c and yield us nothing in every other and that we believe that c would hold only if we don't play this game. The value to us of playing the game should be the utility of gaining nothing. On the Bernoulli analysis, however, the value is the weighted average of the utilities of gaining five dollars and of gaining nothing, the weights being the probabilities of c and of *not-c,* and this is almost certainly greater.

The new wrinkle is that the options here bear differently probability-wise on these contexts, that the probability of each context varies with whether we think we will or won't play. We can provide for this complication by making a now-common adjustment. This says that the probabilities that figure in our evaluation of an option are our *conditional* probabilities, the condition being our taking that option. But what are conditional probabilities?

What is the probability that someone sets, say, on k conditionally on h? We cannot make it the probability he *would* set on k if he believed h, for that is something only contingent, and a person's expected utilities reflect just the actual states he is in. Still, if he would in fact set the probability x on k if he believed h, he is now in a linked actual state, the state of being disposed to degree x to believe k if he believed h. We will say that this partial disposition is his conditional probability in the case.

Again, the probability someone sets on k conditionally on h is his degree of disposition to believe k if he now believed h – strictly: if, in addition to all else he believed, he believed the compatible h. The actualism of this is essential, but the linkage of the contingent and the actual lets us speak of conditionals (indirectly) in the usual would-if terms. Note that, on the analysis here, every probability is conditional, if only in a vacuous

47

way, a person's apparent *un*conditional probabilities being conditional on all he believes. (Where all I now believe is b, the unconditional probability I set on k – my degree of belief in k – is my degree of disposition to believe k if I believed b.)

Let $p(k,h)$ be the probability set on k conditionally on h. Let $u(h)$ be the utility of h. Where h reports the option at issue and $o_{h,k}$ reports the outcome of taking it in context k, $u(o_{h,k})$ is the utility of that outcome. That is, $u(o_{h,k})$ is the utility of what the agent thinks would follow from his taking h in this context. So expectedness can be put like this, as Principle 1:

$$u(h) = p(k,h)u(o_{h,k}) + p(m,h)u(o_{h,m}), \qquad (1)$$

given that $p(k\text{-}\&\text{-}m,h) = 0$, that is, that k and m are exclusive for the agent on the condition that h. (This refers to two contexts only, to k and to m, but can be made to cover more.)

The usual way of putting it is different. The principle of expectedness is usually held to be

$$u(h) = p(k,h)u(h\,\&\,k) + p(m,h)u(h\,\&\,m), \qquad (2)$$

given that $p(k\text{-}\&\text{-}m,h) = 0$. We will take (1) to be basic, but (2) is certainly binding too. The two are equivalent where the utilities set on the outcomes of h in certain contexts are the utilities set on the conjunctions of h and the reports of those contexts holding. That is, (1) and (2) are equivalent where

$$u(h\,\&\,k) = u(o_{h,k}) \quad \text{and} \qquad (3)$$
$$u(h\,\&\,m) = u(o_{h,m}),$$

and we will therefore accept (3) too. This last is a principle of going by outcomes – more formally, of *consequentialism*.

The expected utility of h is its utility proper put as a weighted average of certain others. To be guided by expectedness is thus to be guided by the utilities proper, to be inclined to go for the option that has the greatest utility, though only insofar as the utilities of the options are related *via* (1) to other utilities and to certain probabilities. We have in (1) a principle of the hang-together of utilities and probabilities, a principle of their *coherence*. Or we might put it this way, that one mark of a person's being *consistent* is that the utilities and probabilities he sets jointly satisfy (1).

There are other principles like that of expectedness, other principles of the coherence of mental states. These too are also conditions of a person's being self-consistent. The basic principles of probability are these:

$$p(h,k) \geqslant 0, \tag{4}$$

$$p(T,k) = 1, \quad \text{where } T \text{ is any logical truth,} \tag{5}$$

$$p(h\text{-}or\text{-}m,k) = p(h,k) + p(m,k), \quad \text{given that, if the} \tag{6}$$
$$\text{agent believed } k, \text{ he would believe}$$
$$not\text{-}both\text{-}h\text{-}and\text{-}m, \quad \text{and}$$

$$p(h\text{-}\&\text{-}m,k) = p(h,k) \times p(m,k\text{-}\&\text{-}h). \tag{7}$$

Principle 4 is a common convention. We need to posit Principle 5 only for certain exceptional cases; in the usual case, we have (9), from which (5) follows (put T for h in (9)). Principle 6 is the special *addition* principle. (What makes it "special" is the proviso about believing *not-both-h-and-m*.) Principle 7 is the general *multiplication* principle. A useful corollary is

$$p(not\text{-}h,k) = 1 - p(h,k). \tag{8}$$

This follows from (5) and (6) when *not-h* is put for *m*.

A principle of conditional probabilities can be got from (7) for any person who has some (any) belief. Let $p(h)$ be the *un*conditional probability of h, that is, the probability of h conditional on all that the agent believes. In (7), put h for m, k for h, and T for k. Where this person holds at least one belief, $p(h\text{-}\&\text{-}k,T) = p(h\ \&\ k)$ and $p(k,T) = p(k)$. Where also $p(k) \neq 0$, we have

$$p(h,k) = p(h\ \&\ k)/p(k). \tag{9}$$

We will need an analogous principle for the agent's utilities. As above, let $u(h)$ be the utility set on h, its *un*conditional utility, or better, its utility conditional on all that the agent believes.

Let $u(h,k)$ be the utility of h conditional on k. That is, let it be the agent's degree of disposition to want h if, in addition to all else he believed, he believed the compatible k. We now have this principle of conditional utilities:

$$u(h,k) = u(h \mathbin{\&} k). \tag{10}$$

We get (10) from (2) when *not-k* is put for m. If the agent believed k, $p(k,h)$ would be *1* (this by (9)) and $p(\textit{not-k},h)$ would be *0* (by (8)). So if he believed k, the right side of (2) would come down to $u(h \mathbin{\&} k)$: if he believed k, $u(h)$ would equal $u(h \mathbin{\&} k)$. It follows from the linkage of the actual and the contingent that the degree of his disposition to want h if he believed k is $u(h \mathbin{\&} k)$.

Let us note still another possible formulation of expectedness:

$$u(h) = p(k,h)u(h,k) + p(m,h)u(h,m), \tag{11}$$

where, again, $p(k\text{-}\&\text{-}m,h) = 0$. Given (10), this is equivalent to (2) and so may seem redundant. But a special virtue of (11) will emerge in Chapter 3.

Now for some principles of beliefs and desires. Two principles of *noncontradiction:* if a person believes h, he does not believe *not-h*, and if he wants h, he does not want *not-h*. Two principles of *deductive closure:* a person believes every deductive consequence of (the conjunction of) all he believes, and he wants every deductive consequence of (the conjunction of) all he wants. A third principle of closure is this: if a person wants h and believes k, then if m follows from *h-and-k* and nothing follows from m that follows from k alone, he also wants m. (We need the and-nothing-follows-from clause to avoid the implication that he wants all he believes.)

Finally, some principles of *substitutivity*. From deductive closure we get the following: where h and k are logically equivalent, if a person believes h, he also believes k, and if he wants h, he also wants k. We also need this, which is independent of closure: where h and k are logically equivalent, $p(h) = p(k)$

and $u(h) = u(k)$, and for every such h and k and every m, $p(h,m) = p(k,m)$ and $p(m,h) = p(m,k)$ and $u(h,m) = u(k,m)$ and $u(m,h) = u(m,k)$.

More might be said on these matters, but this is all that we need. In Chapter 3, we will make some changes. Those will be corrective provisos; they will be formally marginal. But they will be philosophically central.

2.9 IDEALIZATION

The principles here are familiar. Still, why should we accept them (or their final versions to come)? One answer is that they spell out our concept of mental states being in good working order, our concept of a person's being consistent. If someone violates noncontradiction, if he believes h and also believes *not-h*, we take his thinking to be disordered: we say he reveals incoherence. So too if someone violates any of the other principles noted.

We might also consider a second approach to the question. Let us return to what we have said about beliefs and desires and the rest, that the nature of these mental states is implicit in our theory of reasons, that the theory puts constraints on what (we might think) they are like. Beliefs and desires are states that play a causal role in action, and probabilities and utilities are states that establish what we come to want. Can we now pin these down further? Can we say that beliefs and desires are states of which closure and noncontradiction hold, that probabilities are states of which addition and multiplication hold, etc.? Could we say that our principles of coherence contribute to the shaping of our concepts of mental states (not just, as on the preceding idea, of our concept of their being well ordered)?

If we were asking about the mental states of consistent people only, the answer would be *yes* – by definition. But the question is about thinking in general, about every person's mental states. I incline to say *yes* even here, though all the facts seem against it. None of us is always consistent. We don't believe every deductive consequence of all that we believe, and we don't want every consequence of all that we now want. Our utilities don't always comport with expectedness, our probabilities don't always add up as they should, etc. If we took their being coherent to be definitive of mental states, we would have to deny all this. Or rather, we would have to reject the usual ascriptions of beliefs and the rest to people. There wouldn't be any such states at all, no beliefs or desires or the like, for there are no states that fully satisfy our principles. The principles we have would give us a theory about a set of mere fictions.[47]

One response is to concede that the principles are idealizations and then to make a distinction. A principle that is a *Platonic* idealization speaks of rarefied states and structures to which reality approximates. It is about these states and structures. In an idealization of such a sort, we refer to what doesn't exist (to perfect gases and frictionless planes) but sometimes closely matches what does. In an *Aristotelian* idealization, we abstract from reality differently. Here we speak of what does exist but refer only obliquely to it, describing it as we think it would be in some special circumstances. In the interests of a simple theory, we turn our backs on certain factors that would blur the picture. We say of this or that kind of infection that it causes a fever though we know that the fever can be prevented. We say that inflation encourages spending though we know that other factors work against it. Platonic idealizations express relations that hold between mere fictions. Not so with the Aristotelian ones; infections and fevers and inflation and spending are all real enough.

The point now is that our principles of coherence are idealizations of the Aristotelian sort. They abstract from certain independent, perturbational causal factors. They shape our concepts

---

47 This conclusion is in fact drawn, and just on these grounds, by Daniel Dennett. See his "Intentional Systems" in his *Brainstorms* (Cambridge, Mass.: MIT Press, 1978).

of the mental states that people are in where these factors are absent. A person believes every deductive consequence of all that he believes – but only insofar as he is not distracted or careless or drunk or can't work it out. A person's utilities reflect expectedness, but not if he is emotionally overwrought, etc. This has an up-side and also a down-side. The argument for the fictiveness of beliefs and the rest collapses (if fevers are real, then so are beliefs), but there is a price to be paid: the principles cannot be thought to be true. They are themselves approximations. The constraints they set on beliefs and the rest turn out to be too strong. It may well be that they will be weakened in some way in the future.[48]

A second response is not to wait – to weaken them right now. This might be done by a fuller mentalizing of them, that is, by turning the principles into conditionals whose antecedents cite mental states only. We would then have this: if a person believes *h* and *believes that h* implies *k*, he believes *k*. Also, if he wants *h* and *believes that h* implies *k*, he then wants *k*. Also, if *he believes that* the right-hand side of the equation in (1) equals *x*, the utility he sets on *h* is *x*, etc. Would these weaker principles be descriptively correct? That depends on whether the noise factors work by blocking the beliefs just built in, on whether the new belief conditions provide against all perturbations. If it ever happened that a person believed *h* and also believed that *h* implies *k* and yet (because of, say, resistance or fear) didn't believe *k*, we would still not be done. And of course this does sometimes happen. So the new principles still aren't right, though they stand up a bit better than the others.[49]

48 The two preceding paragraphs derive from Jerry A. Fodor's "Three Cheers for Propositional Attitudes" in his *Representations* (Cambridge, Mass.: MIT Press, 1981).
49 Sturdier (but less useful) revisions are proposed by Christopher Cherniak, who suggests putting "some" in place of "every" in our closure principles and making like changes in the others; see his *Minimal Rationality* (Cambridge, Mass.: MIT Press, 1986).

Either way will do. We could accept the usual principles and note that they are Aristotelian idealizations and don't fully square with the facts. Or we could mentalize these principles (as above) on the grounds that the mentalizations fit better. The two different sets of principles express slightly different ideas of consistency, and our philosophical preconceptions will incline us one way or the other. I will be keeping to our initial set (pending some alterations in that), but the reader may choose for himself.

The reader may be unwilling to choose. He may decline to do any business with what are mere approximations. However, if so, he should reflect that he will have trouble with much of science, even with the principles of mechanics. These last hold only in the absence of friction, only where levers are totally rigid, only where a fall is through a vacuum, etc., and those conditions never are met. Strictly speaking, for *real* levers, etc., the principles are false. Yet this makes them none the less useful because we can make the allowances needed, because we know how to use them. If their departure from the full messy truth doesn't discredit these classical principles, neither can their departure from it discredit our principles here.

3

A MISSING FACTOR

WE started with one of Orwell's experiences in the Spanish Civil War. Orwell was in Spain to help in the fight against Fascism there. He took this to mean that he had to shoot Fascists. On the occasion he is writing about, a Fascist appeared but Orwell didn't shoot, this because the man was half naked. He says he didn't "feel like shooting" him. A man exposed in his private parts is just a man, not a Fascist; he cannot be seen as anything but a fellow human being. At least that was Orwell's report of it, and his account of why he didn't shoot.

Our subject here is not war but logic. Can any proper sense be made of Orwell's not shooting this man? Does Orwell himself make sense of it? How would Aristotle, the founder of logic, have taken to Orwell's explanation? I think he would have endorsed it. Orwell notes that the incident was "the sort of thing that happens all the time," and Aristotle would have agreed there too. He held that the "sort of thing" Orwell mentions occurs in all reasoning and tried to show how. But what he says on the matter is only brief and very obscure.

The theory laid out in Section 2.1 is not the whole of Aristotle's analysis. It is only the part of it that is most frequently cited, that every practical reasoning has two sorts of premises, one sort presenting certain beliefs, the other certain related desires. Aristotle sometimes discusses the logic of practical reasoning differently. He then speaks of two sorts of premises he refers to as *major* and *minor*. On occasion he also describes them as being *general* and *particular*.

55

The major premise presents some bottom-line desire of the agent's. The desire presented is bottom-line in this sense, that what the agent wants in the case plus what he believes entails nothing else that he wants. If this person wants x, believes that x-*only-if-y*, and wants y, his wanting x is not bottom-line for him. Wanting to fight Fascism was not bottom-line for Orwell, for his joining the fighting plus what he believed entailed that he shoot Fascists, and he wanted that too. This last *was* bottom-line: his shooting Fascists plus what he believed entailed nothing else that he wanted. Still, it failed as a major premise.

Suppose that the agent's desire for y is in fact bottom-line for him. Does it make for a major premise? Will he now act on this desire? Or rather, will he now act on that plus his belief that he could bring y about? Aristotle holds that he will act on it only where a certain other premise holds. This other, *minor* premise reports that the agent sees his action as being of the y-sort here, that he sees it as an instance of y'ing. It says that he sees what he thinks he could do as a way of getting something he wants – what the (thus installed) major premise says that he wants. The agent's minor premise is more "particular" than the major. It connects that more "general" premise, which reports his wanting to act in some manner, with the particularity of some option he has, as he himself understands it.

Aristotle puts it this way:

> . . . [J]udgment and understanding and practical wisdom . . . deal with ultimates, i.e. with particulars. . . . Now all things which have to be done are included among particulars or ultimates, for not only must the man of practical wisdom know particular facts, but understanding and judgment are also concerned with things to be done, and these are ultimates. . . . [T]he intuitive reason involved in practical reasonings grasps the last and variable fact, i.e. the minor premise. For these variable facts are the starting points for the apprehension of the end, since the universals are reached from the particulars; of these therefore we must have perception, and this perception is intuitive reason.[1]

1 Aristotle, *Nichomachean Ethics*, 1143a.

There is no denying that this is obscure. Fortunately, there is a helpful "paraphrase *cum* translation" of this passage by David Wiggins. Wiggins restates the last two sentences (starting with "The intuitive reason") as follows:

> In its particular variety . . . intuitive reason concerns the most particular and contingent and specific. This is the typical subject matter of the minor premise. . . . For here, in the capacity to find the right feature . . . resides the understanding of the reason for performing an action, its end. For the major premise, and the generalizable concern which comes with it, arises from this perception of the particular. So one must have an appreciation or perception of the particular, and my name for this is intuitive reason.[2]

In Aristotle's unvarnished version, the minor premise reports the agent's special "grasp" or "perception" of some option he has (of some "thing to be done"). Wiggins speaks of the "features" he attends to, of his "appreciation" of its particularity. Both would say that every person's desires and beliefs allow for many major premises, that the agent always has many bottom-line desires ready to be plugged in by him. The grasp he has of some option before him connects with his wanting to take an action defined by the feature he here perceives – thus selecting a major premise from the many that are ready to go. Again: the agent's minor premise expresses a grasp or understanding of some option and his major premise a desire that is activated by that understanding.

Here is Wiggins himself on the subject (in his own words now, not Aristotle's). Where we must act one way or another, our course is not always clear. That is,

> . . . the relevant features of the situation may not all jump to the eye. To see what they are, to prompt the imagination to play upon the question and let it activate in reflection and thought-experiment whatever concerns and passions it should

2 David Wiggins, "Deliberation and Practical Reason," *Proceedings of the Aristotelian Society* 76 (1975/76), p. 47.

activate, may require a high order of situational appreciation. . . . In this . . . and in the unfortunate fact that few situations come already inscribed with the names of all the human
concerns which they touch or impinge upon, resides the cru-
cial importance of the minor premise. . . . [3]

Every practical reasoning has both a major and a minor
premise. How does this square with the belief-and-desire theory
presented in Chapter 2? There is no problem with the major
premise. Say that the agent's reason for y'ing is (in part) his
desire for x and his belief that *x-only-if-y* and that he could bring
y about. Say he wants y and wants nothing else that follows
from y plus all he believes. *I want x* is his desire premise, *I believe
x-only-if-y and that I could bring y about* is his belief premise, and
I want y is his major premise. The major premise is implicit in the
others (that is, assuming closure).

In a special but common case, the major premise *is* one of the
others. Here wanting y is bottom-line, but the bottom and top
coincide: the agent wants y and wants nothing else that follows
from y plus what he believes, and y doesn't follow from anything else he wants plus what he believes. The desire premise is
I want y. The belief premise is *I believe y-only-if-y and that I could
bring y about*. The major premise is *I want y*, the same as the
desire premise. Again, we have nothing new.

What about the minor premise? The agent thinks he could
bring about y, that y'ing is now an option for him. But not only
must he have this belief; he must, says Aristotle, also see or
understand some option as a y'ing. The minor premise reports
that he does, that he understands (or grasps or sees) some option
as a bringing about of y. This premise adds a new factor, and thus
the premises are of three sorts; they express three sorts of states.
A person's reasons are composed of beliefs, desires, and understandings. To explain why someone brought about y, we need

---

3 Ibid., pp. 43–4. Wiggins speaks of what "should" be activated and of "right"
and "relevant" features. We will put off the question of rightness until the
final chapter.

to note that he wanted some x and believed that x-*only-if-y* and that he could bring y about. We need to note too that he saw some option as a bringing about of y.

A word may perhaps be in order about the difference between reasons and reasonings. Major premises and minor premises are part of the pattern of reasonings, and so are a person's desire premises and his belief premises. These are no part of his reasons – only his beliefs and desires themselves and his understandings are that. His reasonings are his reflections on certain reasons that might now move him and his endorsement of this one or that. They issue in a set of premises reporting or expressing the endorsement he makes, premises saying that, yes, I want *this* and, yes, I believe *that,* etc. One can have reasons without having reasoned, so these two concepts are distinct, and of course too our basic concern is not with reasonings but with reasons. We remark on the minor premises of reasonings because they reveal a new factor of reasons.

Bringing in this new causal factor threatens to complicate things. Why do we need to trouble with it? I hope to show that we couldn't as readily account for people's conduct if we left it out, but this can be put off till later. Here let us just call on Orwell again. Orwell wanted to do what he could to help to defeat Fascism. He believed that this required that he now shoot Fascists and also that the man up ahead was a Fascist and that he thus had an opportunity. Why then didn't he shoot? Because the man's being partly naked kept Orwell from seeing him as the Fascist he was, and without that political mind-set on it, his wanting to shoot Fascists did not connect.

Or we might put it another way. The sight of the other's likeness to himself had brought up old promptings of fellowship, and so he had got on a different track. If his major and minor premises had been: I want to shoot that Fascist and I see I might do it, Orwell would have fired. But the man's pants were down, and Orwell's mind had refocused. He saw that *not* shooting would help a "fellow creature," which connected with his desire to help those "like himself." His minor premise was: I see I might help that fellow, and the major premise: I want to help my fellows. And so he didn't shoot.

Sometimes it is the absence of a suitable understanding that makes for inaction. Think of Sartre's story of the young Frenchman's dilemma. This person wanted to fight for France and also to stand by his mother, and either desire could have made for a major premise for him. However, his options were out of focus. He had no grasp or understanding of them that might have released either inclination (that might have installed either major premise). What held him back, what made for his quandary, was the absence of a fixed understanding. When he finally had things in focus, his course was clear and he could act.

This suggests temporality, that understandings must somehow come first, and Aristotle believed just that. In the quote above (in this section), he says, "[the] variable facts are the starting points for the apprehension of the end," which Wiggins recasts as "the major premise . . . arises from this perception of the particular." Aristotle is speaking of the *course* of a reasoning, of "starting points," of what "arises" from what. But let us drop temporality, and indeed reasoning too. All that is off to the side of what I think is Aristotle's main idea, which is not about *how* people reason but about what their reasons are like. His basic thesis is not about reasoning but about the structure of reasons. It is that reasons involve understandings, that there are no reasons without them. And this is a rich and important idea on which I want to expand.

3.2 DOUBLE ASPECTS

We have remarked on Pascal's priority in the solution of the problem of points and on his role in the first presentation of the expectedness principle. A case can be made for his being a pioneer in another way too. His famous atheist's wager shows how a person might cope with uncertainty where he has no probabilities to go by.[4] Pascal applied himself to our subject in still another connection, though here as a hostile critic only.

In 1656, his friend Arnauld was called up for censure before the University of Paris. Arnauld had held that, because of the sin of Adam, all human action is necessarily evil, but that sometimes, by the grace of God, we can be disposed to act rightly, and so against our nature. These were dangerous Augustinian theses; they smacked of Calvin and Protestantism. Arnauld made it even worse by saying that whatever grace God grants, God can also revoke, that no one can count on God's favor. He said that St. Peter himself lacked grace when he denied knowing Jesus. The effect was like that of an American politician saying that George Washington was a communist. Arnauld was in deep trouble.

Pascal came to Arnauld's assistance with a polemic in the form of a letter; when Arnauld lost, he continued with more.[5] The point was to skewer the Jesuits, who had been Arnauld's opponents. In Letter 2, Pascal reports his going to study with an old Jesuit monk. The heart of the instruction he gets is reached in Letter 7, where the talk is of moral counseling. Here the monk explains the Jesuit "grand method of *directing the intention,*"[6] a new way of turning the mind from thoughts of sin and evildoing. He says that the method

> . . . consists in [a person's] proposing to himself, as the end of his actions, some allowable object. Not that we do not endeavor, as far as we can, to dissuade men from doing things forbidden; but where we cannot prevent the action, we at least purify the motive, and thus correct the viciousness of the means by the goodness of the end. Such is the way in which our fathers have contrived to permit those acts of violence to which men

4 For the wager, see Pascal's *Pensées* (New York: Random House, 1941), pp. 79–84.
5 The letters collectively came to be known as *The Provincial Letters*. My references will be to the Modern Library Edition (New York: Random House, 1941).
6 Ibid., p. 403.

usually resort in vindication of their honor. They have no
more to do than to turn off their intention from the desire
of vengeance, which is criminal, and direct it to a desire
to defend their honor, which, according to us, is quite
warrantable.[7]

A number of other applications follow. The subject of usury
having come up, the monk condemns it. No one may ever lend
money to get interest. However, a Mohatra deal is different; if
the lender intends a Mohatra, he is in the clear. Pascal has never
heard of a Mohatra. The monk explains that it "is effected by the
needy person purchasing some goods at a high price and on
credit, in order to sell them over again, at the same time and to
the same merchant, for ready money and at a cheap rate,"[8] that
is, for less than he owes for them. Since buying and selling is not
itself wrong, a deal of this sort cannot be faulted.

Another application of the monk's "grand method." Suppose
that a

> ... person asks a soldier to beat his neighbor, or to set fire to
> the barn of a man that has injured him. The question is,
> whether ... the person who employed him to commit these
> outrages is bound to make reparation ... for the damage that
> has followed? My opinion is, that he is not. For none can be
> held to restitution, where there has been no violation of jus-
> tice; and is justice violated by asking another to do us a favor?[9]

Here is just one more. May a judge accept a bribe? He may
accept no inducement to decide in any way, but he may take
some money from the party that is in the wrong. "Justice ... is
a debt which the judge owes, and therefore he cannot sell it; but
he cannot be said to owe injustice, and therefore he may law-
fully receive money for it."[10] So if a judge understands the offer
as an inducement to issue some verdict, he may not accept it,
but he is free to accept the money as payment for the services his
verdict will render, though only if the verdict will be unjust.

7 Ibid., p. 404.   8 Ibid., p. 423.   9 Ibid., p. 425.   10 Ibid., p. 429.

These twistings and turnings boggle the mind. Pascal himself was revolted by them. He saw them to be a kind of fraud, an invitation to self-indulgence. Any crime could be dressed up by them, every action approved. The Jesuits smoothed the path to vice and eased the conscience afterward. At least that was Pascal's view of the matter, and he let it go at that. He didn't press the question of how the Jesuits reached their conclusions. He didn't see any need to.[11]

What let the Jesuits think as they did? Their theory rested on two planks, neither of them solid. The first plank was philosophical; it was the old rule of *double effect* – "double aspect" would have been better, or even "double description." The rule says this, that where the same action might be described in several ways and only one of them reports the intention the agent had in taking it, then just that description is relevant to a judgment of the moral status of the action.[12] The second plank is the supposition of the "directability" of intentions, the idea that a person can choose the intention that will move him to act.

No doubt the double-aspect rule was too strong (too permissive). Still, something like it, suitably weakened, has to be correct. Perhaps an acceptable rule would say only that a person's intentions matter, that our moral judgments of his conduct must take some account of them. Here we may have to part with Pascal, who appears to reject even this. He speaks with approval of those "austere moralists" for whom nothing mattered except what the agent brought about, who looked at what happened, regardless of *why*. Such austerity ignores motivation and so is too strong in the opposite way (too impersonal, too austere).

---

11 There are grounds for thinking that he was not playing fair. For a strongly partisan rebuttal, see James Brodrick, S. J., *The Economic Morals of the Jesuits* (London: Oxford University Press, 1934).

12 This doctrine first appears in Aquinas; see his *Summa Theologica*, Pt. II-II, Quest. 64, Art. 7. For its development, see Albert R. Jonsen and Stephen Toulmin, *The Abuse of Casuistry* (Berkeley: University of California Press, 1988), pp. 221ff.

If we allow intentions at all, we must consider the second plank. This says that our intentions are up to us, that we can "direct" them at will, though the thesis went deeper. A person's intentions reflect his understandings, and it was these that were thought up to him. The Jesuits took understandings to be sorts of inner torches – today we might speak of flashlights. A person can point the beam of his flashlight at whatever he wants to see. He can have it light up any side or surface of what is before him. Likewise, in the beam of his understanding, a person can see any action he takes however he wants to see it. He can see it as prompting someone to commit a crime or as asking him for a favor, as accepting an inducement to reach a certain verdict or as taking payment for services.

The metaphor of the flashlight is poor, much as the similar metaphor of beliefs and desires as inner switches is poor. Beliefs and desires can't be switched on and off to serve our needs or convenience, though, over time, we can sometimes change them. If we want to stop wanting to smoke, we go to Smoke Enders, or hire a hypnotist, or have ourselves marooned on an island. Our beliefs are less pliable to our wills, but, over time, they too can be bent.[13] So, if we work hard enough at it, we can, in the long run, reshape our understandings. But we can't manage that in a wink, when and how we want. The Jesuits held to the contrary, which makes them now sound glib.

The Jesuits spoke of self-direction as a simple and effortless matter, and they are not alone in this. Many of their critics do just the same. These others agree that intentions are directable, that our understandings are up to us, but they contend that an ethics of intentions is for that very reason a sham: all we need do is to shift our understanding from *this* to *that* and we can act as we please. Again, self-direction is never that easy. A person can't change his understandings whenever he wants them to change. He cannot change how he sees things at will any more than he can change his beliefs.

13 Pascal himself shows how in one case; see his *Pensées*, p. 83.

Consider the arsonist in the monk's example. We are told he might see his action as "I set that house on fire" or as "I do my friend a favor." The Jesuit moralists seem to have held that, by seeing it as a favor, he could avoid all guilt. The critics respond that this just reveals the emptiness of the double-aspect rule. Both sides take for granted that it is up to the arsonist how he now sees his action. This gets the picture wrong from the start. A real-life arsonist is likely to see it simply as being arson and cannot change the way that he sees it because that would suit him – he can't change his intention. So he cannot use the rule to get himself declared blameless, and the critics can't complain that the rule has no bite.

Pascal's contempt for the Jesuits' ethics kept him from reflecting on their idea of intentions. It kept him from asking what intentions might be and how the intentions that people have relate to what they do. In our terms here, the answer is this, that an intention is an operative desire, one that is making for action, that an intention is a desire of the agent's made effective by his understanding. Or we could put it in Aristotle's terms, that an intention is the desire expressed by the agent's major premise, a bottom-line desire grounded in his view of some option he has.

There is nothing new for our theory in the concept of people's intentions. Every intention is a desire, though not all desires are intentions. Still, perhaps we should pause for a moment. Since intentions are kinds of desires, our logic of desires may need some more work. Are there any special constraints on what might serve as a person's intentions? This was not a question that either the Jesuits or Pascal ever raised, but a famous philosopher soon raised it. He held that intentions (or what are much like them) are governed by a distinctive principle of logic.

3.3 ADDING TO LOGIC

The philosopher was Kant, and the new constraining principle was his generalization principle. Kant speaks of the *maxim* by which an action is determined. An action is right only if its maxim can be generalized. More fully, no action is right unless its maxim is one on which the agent could wish all people to act: "I am never to act otherwise than so that I could also will that my maxim should become a universal law."[14] Here we are still in ethics, but, in Kant's eyes, this basic principle is a principle of rationality. The basis of his ethics is the logic of coherence.

What is the maxim of an action? Kant is not very helpful here. He describes a maxim as "a subjective principle of action, . . . the principle on which the subject acts,"[15] but this remains unclear, for what does he mean by a "subjective principle"? Kant's examples are a mixed bag: to kill myself when living longer is likely to bring me misery, to lie when I find it convenient, to make a promise I cannot keep when that offers me benefit, to neglect my talents, to gain material advantage. These suggest that a person's maxim is not his whole reason for doing what he does, nor any part of that reason. The maxim is rather what he wants to do, or the action-sort involved, "the character of the action taken by itself,"[16] or the action in the context it has (e.g., "when living longer is likely to bring me misery"). But how then is the maxim "subjective," and how does the agent "act on" it?

Kant leaves all this very vague, so we must take up the slack for him. Let me suggest he had this in mind, that a person's maxim is what he wants to do and then does, what he wants to do at some bottom level of desire, though only where the desire is effective, where it leads the agent to act. Thus it is his action itself under the aspect his view of it grasps – this last being what makes for the subjectivity involved. Kant speaks of the maxim *of an agent* (this we have just considered) and also of the maxim *of an action:* the maxim *of an action* is the aspect under which the agent views it. The maxims on which a person acts are of the

14 Immanuel Kant, *Fundamental Principles of the Metaphysics of Morals* (New York: Liberal Arts Press, 1949), p. 19.

15 Ibid., p. 38.

16 Kant, *Lectures on Ethics* (New York: Harper & Row, 1963), p. 44.

former sort: to *act on* some maxim one has is to act on the desire defining that maxim.[17]

The test of rightness that Kant proposes has to do with the concept of maxims. Suppose you are thinking of suicide and see it simply as killing yourself. Perhaps your suicide would please your relatives and perhaps you are amiable and want to please them. Still, their pleasure is an extra for you, not the object you have in view, so your maxim is to kill yourself; it isn't to do what pleases these others. Your killing yourself and your doing what pleases them are in brute fact the same event, but it is your seeing it as a self-killing that, for Kant, makes it wrong. You can certainly want all people to do what pleases their relatives. You can't want them all to kill themselves – you can't want your maxim generalized. Again, Kant's test applies to maxims, not to actions *tout court*.

We could have put "intentions" in the place of "maxims" here, and this suggests that Kant's position is in some ways like that of the Jesuits. Kant and the Jesuits agree in holding that the rightness or wrongness of an action depends on how the agent sees that action: the self-same right action under a different maxim (different intention) might have been wrong. How far can this likeness be pressed? Was Kant just a closet Jesuit?

Critics of Kant often say that any action will pass for him. Whatever anyone wants to do can be dressed up to look alright; the agent can always invent a maxim that would do the job. This was the line that the Jesuits took, but it wasn't Kant's. The agent's motivation is not up to him. He can always invent a maxim (imagine it), but he can't make it *his*. He cannot make himself act on it. And only a maxim he acts upon is a true maxim of his conduct.

---

17 A useful discussion of Kant's concept of maxims appears in Onora Nell (O'Neill), *Acting On Principle* (New York: Columbia University Press, 1975), Chap. 3. See also her "Consistency in Action" in her *Constructions of Reason* (Cambridge University Press, 1989).

Suppose that I covet your letter opener and find an opportunity of walking off with it. My maxim would be to steal this thing. Ought I to act on that maxim? Kant would say *no*, for I can't want it generalized: I cannot want everyone acting on it. But mightn't I change my maxim? Mightn't I see the action somehow that would allow for generalization, see it perhaps as adding to my collection of fancy letter openers? The first point is that I might but I can't – I can't change my seeings at will. A second point is that the *mights* here don't matter. The maxim of my action reflects my perspective; it expresses my current understanding. I now have the maxim I have, and the principle applies to that only. The fact that my maxim might have been different has no bearing whatever.

Let us turn to the principle itself. What maxims does it rule out? Suppose that I want to kill myself, to do it as soon as I can. If everyone always killed himself as soon as he could do it, no one would ever have lived to reach puberty. No child would ever have been conceived, and no one would have been born. A person cannot kill himself unless he first is born. So I can't want my maxim generalized, for I would then want a contradiction (or something very close to it).

But this supposes that my maxim is to kill myself *as soon as I can*. Let it be instead to kill myself *when living longer is likely to bring me misery*, the maxim in Kant's own example. Would acting on that be alright? There would be no contradiction in everyone's acting on it. And what about the maxim to steal? If everyone always stole all he could, no one would ever own what he had, and without property there can be no theft. But let my maxim be to steal *what I want* – not to steal all in sight. If everyone always acted on that, the institution of property needn't collapse and theft, within limits, could continue. Does that now let me steal? If you can't want your maxim generalized, then you oughtn't to act on it. But many maxims of stealing pass the generalization test. So also do many maxims of murder, of rape, etc.

This is a common critique, but Kant would say that it misses his point. In order for me to be able to want my maxim to be generalized, it isn't enough that the generalization not be contradictory. It is also necessary that *my wanting it* not be self-defeating.[18] Let *h* report that everyone acts on some maxim I have. It isn't enough for *h* to pass muster: *my wanting h* must qualify too, and here we approach something new.

Kant implies that my desires must satisfy not only the principles of noncontradiction and closure but also another of a different sort. He does not present that new basic principle or even say much about it. Reflexivity is somehow involved: my wanting nothing does not affront logic but *I want to want nothing* does. We have here a principle that denies me certain desires because they would be *mine*, because it would go counter to logic if those desires were had *by me*. (The like has been said to hold for beliefs. It may be true that I believe nothing, and you are free to believe that. But *I* am not free to believe it, for *I believe that I believe nothing* reports something self-defeating.)

This leaves us with a question. What must I and *h* be like for *I want h* to be self-defeating? Why, in particular, is it self-defeating if I want everyone to steal what he wants – or to take a bribe, or to burn someone's house? Kant hints that the answer depends in some way on certain other things I want, but consistency isn't enough. Suppose I established consistency by dropping some of those *other* desires; Kant would still refuse to endorse my killing and stealing, etc. So we have little to go on. The logic of self-defeat is left dark.

Let us set all this aside. Kant's idea of the maxims of conduct was independent of it. Indeed, the concept of people's maxims soon had a busy life of its own, having been taken up by others who put it to various uses. Several distinctive schools of philosophy developed in Germany in the nineteenth century on this

---

18 Kant is explicit on this; see his *Fundamental Principles of the Metaphysics of Morals*, p. 41.

basis, schools of the "Geisteswissenschaften," and these in turn were followed by schools of "hermeneutical" thought. Kant's own thinking figured little here. The project was to study not the rightness of conduct but its intelligibility, and the work was less Kantian in spirit than antipositivist and antiscientific. A number of concepts of people's intentions and understandings were introduced, many of them in discussions rejecting the possibility of causal explanations of behavior.[19]

We can set aside these anticausal analyses too. They no longer find much support, at least they find very little support on the English-speaking scene, where the followers of Wittgenstein waved the hermeneutical flag for a while.[20] Still, the central idea remains. Kant's idea of the "subjective" element survives both the vagueness of his generalization test and the decline of the animus against causes. It survives because it brings out a basic factor of practical reason. It is yet another way of noting the agent's seeings or understandings.

The concept of people's maxims depends on that of their understandings. But on that topic, we are still on square one. The question is, what *are* understandings? This recalls the questions we asked in Chapter 2 about probabilities and utilities, which connected with the same questions about beliefs and desires. I could offer no definitions of these, no one-by-one reductions of them, and I can offer no simple definition of understandings either.

The nature of beliefs and desires and the rest must be grasped all together. It comes out in a theory of mind, in what such a theory says about them. In part it appears in a theory of reasons, in how that says they combine to make for action. The case is no different for understandings. Here too the analysis we want is

19 See Georg Henrik von Wright, *Explanation and Understanding* (Ithaca: Cornell University Press, 1971), Chap. 1. See also Karl-Otto Apel, *Understanding and Explanation* (Cambridge, Mass.: MIT Press, 1984), Part 1.
20 See, for instance, Peter Winch, *The Idea of a Social Science* (London: Routledge and Kegan Paul, 1958).

implicit in a theory that assigns them a role. The rest of this chapter presents such a theory, a theory of reasons in which understandings figure on a par with beliefs and desires.

3.4 PROPOSITIONS

Wanting and believing can be seen as relations. Let *a* want *h*, or let *a* believe *h*. Then *a* stands in a certain relation to *h*. Here *a* is some person. What sort of an object is *h*?

Suppose that I want some coffee. What is it that I then want? Not some physical substance, or some quantity of it: the coffee itself. What I want has *me* in it somehow. I wouldn't be gratified by any coffee that went to *you*. Also, I don't want the coffee later, and I don't want it poured over my head. What I want is that *I now drink coffee*. But what sort of a thing is that?

It looks as if it might be some action, or at least some event or occurrence. But this can't be the answer either, for I may fail to get that coffee, in which case no event of my drinking it will occur. There is then no action or event for my desire to relate me to. Perhaps we ought to say instead that what I want is a certain *possibility*. But I don't want the mere possibility – I don't just want some event to be possible. What I want is that *the possibility becomes actual*. And the question is, what is this *that*-thing?

I have no satisfactory answer, so we will have to make do without. Since, however, we need a word here, let us refer to the sought-for object as a *proposition*: what a person wants is always some proposition, and what he believes is a proposition too. Also, a person's utilities are set on propositions and so are his probabilities, and conditional utilities and probabilities have proposition *pairs* as their objects.

Again, a proposition isn't an event or occurrence or some mere possibility. Nor is it any linguistic entity like a sentence or a clause. I can report what I want by using different sentences in different languages, and the same sentence (say, "I get some coffee"), in different people's mouths, expresses different propositions. A proposition is the sort of thing that can be either true or false, can be confirmed, deduced, refuted. But this alone says little. It doesn't get us beyond the idea that propositions are the objects of certain relations, of certain mental attitudes, that they are the foci of wantings, believings, hopings, fearings, and the like.

We need not feel sheepish about this. Propositions are being explained, though not in terms of other matters, in terms of events or sentences. They are being accounted for in terms of the role that they play in people's lives. In this, they are like beliefs and desires and probabilities and utilities, of which we make sense in a similar way. The difference is that our functional analysis of beliefs and the rest brings out their causal roles, while propositions are not causal factors. There is nothing they bring about. Their role is to mark off distinct mental states, to individuate the beliefs and desires (and probabilities and utilities) that people have. What distinguishes a person's beliefs (or desires or whatever) is that they focus on different propositions.

Could we *define* propositions as the objects of belief and the like? No, not even if "and the like" were spelled out, however that was done. This because not all propositions are believed or wanted (or the like). There are detached, free-floating propositions, propositions not focused upon by any mental attitude. Say that I want h, and that k follows from h. What follows from a proposition is itself a proposition, but it may be that I don't believe k, or want it or hope for it, and that no one else does either. The proposition k is like any other, though it is not now an object of thought.

Still, we can't leave it at that. Recall that what we utter or write are not propositions but sentences only – perhaps only strings of words. The words put together don't peg a proposition; every proposition can be differently worded. When is a difference just in the words? We spoke of the individuation of beliefs and desires in terms of the propositions focused upon. It would help to be able to say how propositions themselves are distinguished. What individuates propositions? When are we dealing with several of them and when with only one?

Let us consider this idea, that distinct propositions can't be logically equivalent, that those that are equivalent are *ipso facto* the same. This would make it a test of the distinctness of propositions that they do not entail each other. That Jack will marry Jill and that Jill will marry Jack *do* entail each other, and so they are the same proposition. If you believe that Jack will marry Jill, you believe that Jill will marry Jack – it is the same belief. And if you *want* Jack to marry Jill, you want her to marry him. If you want Jack to marry Jill and I want Jill to marry Jack, these are two distinct desires (one of them yours, the other mine), but we want the same thing.

This simple idea will not work: $2 + 2 = 4$ and $3 + 3 = 6$ are equivalent but they are distinct propositions. *All* the truths of mathematics are logically equivalent. If this made them all the same, no one could learn any mathematics after learning that $2 \neq 1$. There would be nothing more to learn. So also outside mathematics proper. *Cats eat mice* is logically equivalent to *cats eat mice and $log_a a = 1$*. If all equivalent propositions were the same, these would be the same proposition. You couldn't believe one and not the other (even if you knew nothing of logs!), not because that would be inconsistent, but because there would be no *one* and the *other* but only a single *one*.

Equivalent propositions are not all the same. We need to go a bit further and say that propositions are made up of concepts, that their concepts are essential to them. New concepts make for new propositions. (When we accept the kinetic theory of heat, the sentence "the sun is hot" expresses a new proposition for us.) This implies that, if their concepts are different, propositions are distinct even where they are logically equivalent. That is: propositions are only the same if they are equivalent and involve the same concepts.[21] The concepts of 2 and 4 are different from those of 3 and 6, so $2 + 2 = 4$ and $3 + 3 = 6$ are different propositions. Likewise with the propositions about the cats and the $\log_a$ of a. This points us in the right direction, though of course it raises new questions. How does a proposition involve its concepts and when are two *concepts* the same? (Is *Jack kissed Jill* the same proposition as *Jill was kissed by Jack* – is the concept of kissing the same as that of being kissed?) These questions can here be left open.

We will bring in another dark matter and speak of what are called *facts*. Let us take a fact to be whatever a true proposition reports, and let us also turn this around and say that a true proposition reports a fact. The proposition that *Jack married Jill* (assuming it true) reports that he married her: it reports that fact. This can be passed over quickly, but note that this way of thinking of facts allows for an asymmetry. Although for every (true) proposition there is just a single fact, any fact can be differently reported by many different propositions. Where two propositions report the same fact, we will say they are *coreportive*. This idea is central to what follows, so we had better get it clear.

When can we say of two propositions that they report the same? Let us start here with the idea of their *material* equivalence, that of their being both true or both false. Not all materially equivalent propositions are coreportive, only those that are equivalent on certain grounds. *London is in England* and *Paris is in France* are materially equivalent, but they are not coreportive. Two propositions that are coreportive are *Martha Custis married George Washington* and *Martha Custis married the Father of his Country;* these two report the same fact. They are coreportive not because they are equivalent but because of how it happens that

21 Having the sameness of propositions depend on the sameness of their constituents derives from an idea developed long ago in the study of the synonymy of sentences. See, for instance, Rudolf Carnap, *Meaning and Necessity,* Enlarged Edition (Chicago: Chicago University Press, 1956), pp. 56–64.

they both are true. The basic idea is this: propositions are core-portive where there are circumstances in the world other than those which they (or their negations) report from which the equivalence of these propositions follows.

This can be expanded a bit. Materially equivalent propositions are coreportive where their equivalence follows from certain physical self-identities, where it follows from self-identities other than any reported by these propositions themselves (or by their negations) – where it follows from *independent* physical self-identities. The two propositions about Martha Custis are coreportive because George Washington *was* the Father of his Country. The equivalence of these propositions follows from this self-sameness, which neither alone reports. (But for the clause about independence, *Washington was the Father of his Country* would be coreportive with *Washington was Washington,* and also with *Washington was the first President,* and even with *Adams was the second;* for all these report self-identities from which together their material equivalence follows.)

Are we not facing another problem of individuation here? We raised the issue of distinctness and sameness regarding proposi-tions. Isn't there also a question about facts, about the self-sameness of what it is that coreportive propositions report? I think we can say that facts are the same if they are reported by coreportive propositions. This no doubt looks circular, but to say that two propositions are coreportive we needn't first find that what they report is the same. Our test of their being coreportive is not the sameness of the facts they report. The test does look to self-sameness, but only to that of *things* or of *people* (like that above of George Washington), and sometimes of *places* or *times* and also of *properties* or *relations* (like that of being married), and sometimes of *events* or *situations.* Here too we might ask what sameness means, but somewhere or other we have to stop, and I think we can stop where we are.

Still, we ought to say a few words about the self-sameness of events and situations. The coreportiveness of propositions sometimes depends on just this. For instance, *he kissed her* and *he kissed her on the cheek* and *he owes a million dollars* and *he owes his aunt a million*. If these propositions are coreportive, it isn't because of any self-sameness of people or things or places or properties but because the facts they report involve the same events or situations. I will hold that events/situations are the same if they have the same causes and effects. Or better, to avoid still more issues of sameness (about these causes and effects), that e and f are the same event/situation where what causes e also causes f and what e causes is caused too by f.[22]

What about false propositions? Our analysis works as well for these. It allows us to say that *Betsy Ross married George Washington* is coreportive with *she married the Father of his Country*. But since she did not marry him, what do these propositions report? On one reading, they report nothing: no facts are reported by false propositions. This threatens to give us some trouble, for if they all report nothing, then each of them reports the same. And that suggests that a false proposition ought to be thought coreportive with every other, that *Betsy Ross married George Washington* is coreportive with *she married George Bush*.

This has to be avoided somehow, so let us speak of *possible* facts, facts that are possible but not actual. We will say that false propositions (with one exception) report possible facts. (The exception is the self-contradiction, which reports nothing, either actual or possible.) Better, we will stretch the word "fact" to cover both actualities and possibilities. This will put true and false propositions on a semantic par for us. It will allow us to say of any proposition (contradictions excepted) that it reports a fact, and of different false propositions that they report different (possible) facts.

Here we meet more questions of sameness, this time about possibilities. Take *he owes a million dollars* and *he owes his aunt a*

---

22 I take this last from Donald Davidson; see his "The Individuation of Events" in his *Essays on Actions and Events*.

million, and suppose that these propositions are false. Are they coreportive? How does our view of the sameness of events apply to merely possible events? Can events that never occur be causes and effects? I will pass these questions by, having no good answers to them. Let me note only that a single possibility, like a single actuality, can be variously reported. *Betsy Ross married George Washington* and *she married the first President* are coreportive; they are two ways in which Betsy's brother may have conceived a certain possibility.

A person may believe (or want or whatever) just one of two coreportive propositions. He might entertain both propositions, but not aware of their being coreportive, disbelieve one though he believes the other. Or he might entertain just the one he believes, the other not even crossing his mind. The concept here is familiar, but let us pause over it anyway. To *entertain* a proposition is to admit it as such, to take it into one's mental orbit, to keep it available for being believed and the like. This acceptance or harboring of propositions is the basic propositional attitude. What makes it basic is that it is presupposed by every other. No beliefs (or desires or whatever) without entertainings: if you don't entertain a proposition, you can take no other attitude toward it.

What about the converse? Could a person entertain a proposition and neither believe it nor want it or the like? Are there *mere* entertainings? It seems to me that there are. You tell me that you dreamt last night that Napoleon had a mole on his thigh, and so I now entertain that proposition. I don't believe it – it was only a dream. Nor do I want it to have been true, or wish that it were, or hope that it was. I only hold it in mind.

A question of a different sort is whether an entertaining is some current awareness. Does entertaining a proposition imply a conscious attendance to it, or can what a person now has in mind just be on his books, having been entered and filed? It isn't clear what this is asking: what kind of a state is awareness? Still, I see no grounds for the thesis that what we entertain must be present to us. However we construe being *aware* or *conscious*, a person need not be currently conscious of all he believes or wants. At no time today, until just now, did I attend to *the Democrats win*. But I wanted their winning this morning no less than I do now, so I must have entertained the idea of their winning this morning too.

Out of sight is not out of mind. But a proposition we now entertain must at some time have been in sight. Otherwise, our entertaining a proposition could just be our knowing a certain sentence, our knowing how to use it. I make good sense of the sentence "My hair has turned bright green." I have known it – known how to use it – for years. But I have never, until this minute, entertained the proposition expressed by it. In fact, I make sense of countless sentences while entertaining propositions much fewer in number. The difference, I think, is this, that we come to know sentences wholesale as we learn a new language (or new words) but can't entertain a proposition unless we first encounter it alone, unless we first face up to it.

What is an *encounter* with a proposition? What is a *facing up* to it? (Or again, what is an *awareness* of it?) I can only give some examples. I first encountered the proposition about my green hair a few minutes ago. I had never *met* it before (never had any awareness of it). Likewise when you told me your dream: that was the first time I met the proposition about Napoleon's mole. Likewise also when I decided to write a paragraph about encountering propositions. I had never before encountered the proposition that I would write such a paragraph.[23]

3.5 UNDERSTANDINGS

A person may be ignorant of some physical self-identity and so not know two coreportive propositions to be coreportive. He

23 For a discussion of entertaining (there are very few), see H. H. Price, *Belief* (London: George Allen and Unwin, 1969), pp. 189–203. (Here entertain-

may then believe one of them true and not believe the other, or want one and not want the other. And that may affect how he chooses and acts. Oedipus, on the day of his wedding, believed he would marry the Queen of Thebes. This proposition he believed (and wanted) was coreportive with that of his marrying his mother. The bad part was that he didn't know this and so didn't believe he would marry his mother. Had he believed it, he would have changed his plans.

Or take the Biblical story of Jephthah returning home from the war. He wanted to make a sacrifice of the first living thing that met him at his door. He had sworn to God he would do this. It turned out he was met by his daughter. What he had come home wanting was coreportive with the proposition that he would kill his daughter. Had he known that earlier, he wouldn't have taken the oath that he took, and he wouldn't then have done what he went on to do.

Oedipus and Jephthah both wanted one but not the other of two coreportive propositions, not knowing them to be coreportive. The same can happen in the fullness of knowledge. Sometimes a person wants just one of two propositions though he knows they are coreportive. Take the case of Orwell in Spain. He knew that *I shoot that Fascist ahead* and *I shoot that fellow creature* were coreportive – they were coreportive because that Fascist *was* that fellow creature. Orwell knew it and yet he wanted the former and not the latter and so put down his gun. Likewise, Sartre's French patriot knew that *I join the army* and *I leave my mother* were coreportive. Joining the army *was* leaving his mother; that was only too obvious. Still, he wanted to join the army (and, it may be, even acted on this) without then wanting to leave his mother, indeed while wanting to stay with her.

ings are mental events: they are only encounters.) See also R. B. Braithwaite, "The Nature of Belief," *Proceedings of the Aristotelian Society* 33 (1932/33), and "Belief and Action," *Proceedings of the Aristotelian Society*, Supp. Vol. 20 (1946).

Let us recall the problem we found these cases raising for the theory of action. It seems that belief-desire pairs don't always move a person to act; we sometimes act on one such pair and don't act on another. The Frenchman wanted to join the army and knew that this meant he had to pack, and perhaps this belief-and-desire led him to pack up and leave. He also wanted to help his mother and knew that this called for his getting a job, but here nothing happened: he looked for no job. Why was he moved in one way and not the other? Orwell wanted to help win the war and knew that this called on him to shoot. Yet he held back. How come?

It will not do to say that the Frenchman wanted to leave more than he wanted to stay, and that Orwell wanted to spare the man more than he wanted to kill him. This would bring in utilities, to which the theory assigns a role only where the agent is conatively uncertain, where he hasn't decided what he wants. The Frenchman and Orwell were not uncertain. They had the settled desires (and beliefs) the usual theory finds sufficient for action. These should have led the Frenchman to leave and also to stay, whatever his utilities, and should have led Orwell to shoot and also not to. Neither of course could act in both ways. What made each act the way that he did and not the other way instead?

The general drift of what I will argue must have been clear for some time. It has to do with how a person relates to the facts reported by what he entertains. We spoke above of his *understandings* of these facts. We said too that he *sees* them somehow – Aristotle spoke of his *grasping* them. Let us now note two sorts of cases. In one sort, the agent entertains a proposition and entertains none that is coreportive with it. No problem in such a case: the proposition the agent entertains expresses the understanding he has. The other sort is more challenging. How does a person understand a fact where (like Orwell and the Frenchman) he entertains several propositions reporting it?

There is no comprehensive answer. Sometimes he understands it as the conjunction of them. My own understanding of Martha's marrying George is just such a conjunction; it links up *she married George Washington, she married the future First President, she married the Father of his Country,* and more. At other times, a person stands back and puts off judgment, as the Frenchman did. Or he may see the fact reported first in one way and then in some other – the Frenchman's predicament on a different day. First one proposition stands out for him, or *strikes* him or *leaps out* at him, and then another stands out. We sometimes speak here of *salience* (from the Latin for "leaping forth"). Or a person may, like Orwell, settle directly in this way or that. No shifting of salience in his case, and no conjoining either: the soldier's being a Fascist was no part of Orwell's view of his shooting him.

There is another possibility still. Where a person isn't aware that two propositions he entertains are coreportive, he lacks an incentive to settle on one (or to conjoin them, or to stand back). What they report he then understands in both these factually equivalent ways, thinking them factually independent. This is not a lapse in logic; all it reveals is a certain ignorance of fact. Compare it with the unlikely case of someone who thinks two propositions coreportive (whether or not they are indeed that) and understands the fact(s) they report in one way and also the other. Here we might say is a logical fault – call it a failure of *univocity.* This last is a kind of incoherence, though not any kind we noted in Chapter 2. (Sometimes univocity functions instead as a constraint on the expression of understandings: if the agent thinks *h* and *k* coreportive and claims that both express his understanding of some fact, we take it to be that his understanding is expressed by *h-and-k.*)

The Frenchman swung between understandings and Orwell settled on one directly, his mind being fixed from the start. But what was being swung between, and what was settled upon? That is, again, what are understandings? The answer will come when we have the whole theory and get a sense of how it applies. But let us take some first steps here by saying what understandings are not.

The basic negative point is this, that they are not beliefs or desires. A person who sees his life as half over may come to see it as half yet to come. No change of beliefs need be involved, not even indirectly, as what caused him to change. Of course, there *may* be a causal nexus. What we believe may affect how we see things (as it often affects what we want), but the two then still are distinct. So also, perhaps, a changed understanding may derive from some change in what is wanted, but the new desire and understanding are then not the same either.

Let me stress the distinction of our beliefs and our understandings, for these very often are run together, the way we understand a certain fact being confused with what we believe about it. Not every proposition that we believe expresses some understanding we have. That is, a person may believe a proposition and yet not see any fact in its terms. Orwell believed that shooting the soldier would bring down a Fascist, an enemy. But he didn't, then and there, see this (possible) fact in that way.

Conversely, if someone has some understanding, he needn't believe the proposition that expresses it. He may be only considering the proposition, reflecting on it, debating it. He may have already rejected it. Orwell understood his shooting the soldier as his killing a man, a "fellow creature," but he then knew that he wouldn't shoot, so he didn't believe he would do it. (He knew he would kill a man *if* he fired, but that is a different proposition.) The beliefs we have may focus on propositions that don't express any understandings we have, and our understandings may be expressed by propositions we do not believe.

This too should be noted about understandings, that, unlike beliefs and desires, they are not propositional attitudes. What a person understands is not any proposition. What he understands is the fact that this or that proposition reports, the fact that some event or situation occurred or held or holds or *might* hold. Orwell had formed a new understanding of the prospect of his shooting the soldier – of that (possible) fact. The Frenchman sought an understanding of his joining the war or of staying home. In an understanding, we map out a fact, we grasp it in terms of some proposition. Still, it is the fact that we grasp, not the proposition, that we then understand.

And of course too, our understandings aren't themselves propositions, though the way we speak may suggest this. We say, "I have come to see that . . . " or even, perhaps, "My understanding is that . . . " and finish this off with a proposition. It may then seem that the proposition *is* our understanding, but this confusion must be resisted. It would identify our understanding of some fact with how it is we understand it. An understanding is a mental state, a grasping or seeing of some fact. It can't be the same as the proposition in terms of which that fact is grasped.

Understandings are not entertainings (these *are* propositional attitudes), but certain points carry over here. Like entertainings, understandings can be tacit. They can be fully unconscious: we needn't be aware of all our understandings and may sometimes even resist admitting to ourselves how we are seeing things.[24] Also, again as with entertainings, there are *mere* understandings. A person then understands some fact in some way, in terms of some proposition, but neither believes nor wants that proposition nor takes any other attitude toward it – no attitude except entertaining. Betsy Ross's brother may have seen a certain possibility as *her marrying George* and yet been totally neutral to this, neither believing nor wanting it, nor regretting it, nor hoping for it.

Understandings and entertainings remain very different mental states. Their relation to action is different. First about entertainings again. Had Oedipus and Jephthah not entertained what

---

24 Some notes on unconscious seeing appear in Theodore Mischel, "Concerning Rational Behaviour and Psychoanalytic Explanation," *Mind* 74 (1965).

they did, they wouldn't have done what they did. Still, the effects of their entertainings were mediated by their desires. If Oedipus hadn't entertained his marrying Jocasta, he couldn't have wanted to do it. And if he hadn't wanted to do it, he wouldn't have got into trouble. If Jephthah hadn't entertained his making that sacrifice, he couldn't have wanted to make it. And it was his wanting to make it that led him to bind himself to it. Their entertainings mattered – they led them to act – but only by virtue of the desires (and beliefs) for which these entertainings provided.

Entertainings play enabling roles only; they provide for having other mental states. Not so with a person's understandings, which can thus matter on their own. That is, a person's understandings can matter independently of his beliefs and desires. We must now look into that.

3.6 REASON REVISED

Orwell had one belief-and-desire that prompted his shooting the Fascist and another that made for *not* shooting him. The Frenchman had one belief-and-desire that prompted his leaving and another that prompted his staying. A person's belief-desire pairs don't always move him to act – they *cannot* always move him. When do they and when don't they?

My answer is that it depends on their context, on their psychological context. Beliefs *cum* desires gain their force from their connection with a third causal factor. This last is the way that the agent understands these or those possible facts. What settled things for Orwell was that he saw his shooting that soldier as the shooting of a "fellow creature." Likewise, the Frenchman was moved in the end by how he then saw what was open to him, by seeing it either as joining the army or as leaving his mother or in some other way. But how exactly does this work? How can the belief-and-desire theory be revised to allow for understandings?

In all the cases discussed in this chapter, the agent's desires were fixed from the start. In such a case, the basic idea (the *starting* idea) is the one in Section 2.1. This says that a person is moved by his desires and by what he believes he must and could do in order to get what he wants. We have here a model of the explanation of action. Let *h* and *k* be propositions. To explain why someone brought about *k*, we need to note only that he wanted *h* and believed *h-only-if-k* and that he believed he could bring *k* about. Or rather, we need to note this and to assume that he was *driven* and *unimpeded*, in one word: *effective*. [25]

How must this be revised? Some room must be found for the agent's understandings, and this is best done in two stages. First we have to take account of how he saw his option of *k*'ing. (Here I just apply the analysis of Section 3.1.) To explain why he did what he did, we need to note that he wanted *h* and believed *h-only-if-k*. Also that he thought he could bring *k* about and that *he understood his action as a bringing about of k*.

Let us put it directly in terms of the reasons a person has for acting. Suppose he wants *h* and believes *h-only-if-k* and that he could bring *k* about. If he sees some option he has as a *k*'ing, he takes that option. His seeing it so is a part of what moves him. Without that part, he has no full reason, and incomplete reasons have no force. Orwell believed that what he wanted called on him to shoot that Fascist and he thought he could do it. But with the half-naked soldier before him, he saw his shooting as the shooting of a fellow man. He didn't see it as the shooting of a Fascist, and so he lacked the full reason for shooting he would have otherwise had.

This will not quite serve. Orwell wanted to help to stop Fascism. He believed that this required that he shoot that Fascist. He must have also believed it required that he shoot the self-same fellow man. He thought he could now do this, and he saw that option he had as the shooting of a fellow man. Why then didn't

25 Recall that these are technical terms; see Section 2.1.

he shoot? Because the soldier's being half-naked changed Orwell's grasp not only of his options but also of his objective. He still wanted to help to stop Fascism, but (at that moment) he saw this project as the killing of his fellow men. And he backed away from that.

So the analysis must be this. Suppose that someone wants *h* and believes *h-only-if-k* and that he could bring *k* about. If he sees some option he has as a bringing about of *k* and (we here add) *understands his objective as a realization of h,* he now takes that option. To explain later why he did it, we need to report the full reason he had: that he wanted *h* and believed *h-only-if-k* and that he thought he could bring *k* about, and that he saw his action as a bringing about of *k* and *saw his objective as a realization of h.*

This will do for the basic case, though some details call for attention, this to keep our house in order. In Section 2.1, we defined *unimpededness* in terms of beliefs and desires: what an unimpeded person wants and thinks he can bring about, he does bring about. Now that we have admitted understandings, this is clearly too strong. Let us say that a person's being unimpeded says only this about him, that where he wants *k* and thinks he can bring it about *and sees some option he has as a k'ing,* he brings *k* about. We defined *drivenness* in terms of deductive closure, and this needs some touching up too – we will get to that in a moment. (Our new concepts of drivenness and unimpededness compose a new concept of *effectiveness.*)

So much for the person whose mind is made up. This person has some settled objective. What now of someone whose mind is still open, who hasn't yet fixed on what he wants? Here the usual theory of action refers to the agent's probabilities and utilities. Can that be left as it stands? What is the role of a person's understandings where he goes by his probabilities and utilities?

Again, the usual theory is that the agent is rational in a certain sense. He comes to want whichever of his options has the greatest expected utility. And the expected utility of an option is the weighted average of the utilities of its outcomes, of its outcomes in different contexts, the weights being the probabilities of these contexts.

Utilities focus on propositions, so this cuts a few corners. With the corners put back, it says that the expected utility of an option is the weighted average of the utilities of *certain propositions* that report its outcomes. But given the existence of coreportive propositions, this now raises a question. Which propositions reporting the outcomes ought to be considered? Let me suggest that we consider just those that report the outcomes *as the agent understands them*, that the expected utility is a weighted average of the utilities of those propositions. Expected utilities so defined depend on the understandings the agent has, and different understandings might establish different expected utilities for him.

In the last chapter, we spoke of a doctor facing a patient whose disease is unclear. The doctor has two options – he can either operate or do nothing – and he thinks that his patient is either of sort *m* or sort *n*. If the patient is an *m*, the operation would cure him; if he is an *n*, he would die. If he is an *m* and nothing is done, he would quickly get worse; if he is an *n* and nothing is done, he would stay as he is. On the usual analysis, the expected utilities of these two courses are the weighted averages of the utilities of their outcomes in the *m*- and *n*-contexts, the weights being the probabilities of the patient's being of sort *m* or sort *n*.

But there are of course different ways of understanding these outcomes. The doctor may understand two outcomes of his operation as *my patient will recover* and *my patient will die*. Or he may know that the patient is a murderer, in which case he may see them as *this murderer will recover* and *this murderer will die*, and there are countless other ways yet in which he might see these outcomes. Since he is likely to set different values on *my patient will recover* and *that murderer will recover*, how he understands this outcome of his acting affects how he values the option that might yield it. So at least if he goes by expectedness (if he is being rational), for then the expected utilities of his options depend on how he understands their outcomes.

This shapes up the theory for cases in which the agent starts undecided. A person still comes to want the option that has the greatest expected utility, but the expected utility of an option is now defined more precisely. It is a weighted average of the utilities of certain specified propositions, of the propositions expressing the agent's understandings of the outcomes. The rest of the theory stays as it was. That is, it stays as it was after we added the clauses about his understandings of his objective and his options.

Note that those clauses allow understandings to be conclusive for action on their own (not just *via* the mediation of some other mental states). *I shoot that Fascist* and *I shoot that fellow human* reported the self-same option. The way that Orwell saw that option led him to put down his gun. Had he seen it the other way, he would have pulled the trigger, and this though all his beliefs and desires remained exactly the same. Our revised theory of reasons for action shows how understandings can matter on their own. It shows how they can be independent factors, coequal to the agent's beliefs and desires.

3.7 COHERENCE REFINED

Orwell wanted to shoot the Fascist but not to shoot that fellow human though he knew the two were the same. The Frenchman wanted to join the army but not to leave his mother though he knew that to join was to leave. So they both went against a principle of closure in Section 2.8, the one that says that if a person wants *h* and believes *k*, then if *m* follows from *h-and-k* (and nothing that follows just from *k* follows from *m*), he also wants *m*. Suppose that they had adhered to this. Then given the desires and beliefs Orwell had, he would have wanted to shoot

that fellow human. Likewise, given his situation, the Frenchman would have wanted what in fact he did not: he would have
wanted to leave.

For some philosophers, this raises no problem. They hold that
these cases only remind us that people sometimes are inconsistent. A consistent person goes by coherence, and that requires
deductive closure. Orwell wanted to shoot the Fascist, so he
should have wanted to shoot that fellow human. (Or since he
did not want the latter, he shouldn't have wanted the former.)
So also for the Frenchman. Since he wanted to join the army, he
should have wanted to leave his mother. (Or perhaps, since he
wanted to stay, he should have wanted *not* to join.) A consistent
person never wants just one of two propositions he believes
coreportive. Had Orwell and the Frenchman been fully consistent, their understandings couldn't have made any difference.

Not everyone will agree with these judgments. Orwell himself, looking back later, does not fault his frame of mind then –
he doesn't call it disordered – and Sartre does not fault his
friend. I see no grounds for finding fault either. Neither Orwell
nor the Frenchman seem to me to have been remiss. They
reasoned and acted as thoughtful people in their situations may
well have done. If their thinking offends our logic, it is our logic
that ought to give way.

We will make it give way a bit by (tentatively) dropping the
closure principle that is causing the trouble here. Consider that
principle dropped. A person who wants h and believes h and n
coreportive need now not want n. This provides for Orwell and
the Frenchman. It puts them both in the clear, but at the cost of
cutting back logic.

We will have to cut back further. Take the case of the doctor
who set different utilities on *my patient will recover* and *that
murderer will recover* though he believed these propositions coreportive. This person, I suggest, was not remiss either, but the
usual logic holds otherwise. To allow for the doctor's position,

we must allow people who think h and n coreportive to set different utilities on them. And Principle 10, that of conditional utilities, requires that the utilities be the same.

Suppose a person thinks h and n coreportive. Then he believes that h is true if and only if n is. Writing this last as *"h-iff-n"* and putting it for k in

$$u(h,k) = u(h \mathrel{\&} k), \tag{10}$$

we get

$$u(h, h\text{-}iff\text{-}n) = u(h \mathrel{\&} h\text{-}iff\text{-}n) = u(h \mathrel{\&} n).$$

With h and n interchanged, we get

$$u(n, n\text{-}iff\text{-}h) = u(n \mathrel{\&} n\text{-}iff\text{-}h) = u(n \mathrel{\&} h) = u(h \mathrel{\&} n).$$

It follows that

$$u(h, h\text{-}iff\text{-}n) = u(n, n\text{-}iff\text{-}h).$$

But since the agent believes *h-iff-n* and so also *n-iff-h*, this comes to

$$u(h) = u(n).$$

In sum, where a person thinks h and n coreportive, the utility he sets on h must be that which he sets on n. Or rather, this follows from Principle 10, the principle of conditional utilities. Since we want to avoid this constraint, we have to drop Principle 10.

We cannot stop even there, for the same constraint is also imposed by Principle 2 (recall that (2) implies (10)). Put *h-iff-n* for k and *not-(h-iff-n)* for m in

$$u(h) = p(k,h)u(h \mathrel{\&} k) + p(m,h)u(h \mathrel{\&} m). \tag{2}$$

Since the agent believes *h-iff-n*, $p(h\text{-}iff\text{-}n, h) = 1$ (this by (9)), and so $p(not\text{-}(h\text{-}iff\text{-}n), h) = 0$ (by (8)). Principle 2 thus says that $u(h) = 1 \times u(h \mathrel{\&} h\text{-}iff\text{-}n) + 0$, which comes to $u(h) = u(h \mathrel{\&} n)$. Doing this over with h and n interchanged, we find that $u(n) = u(n \, \partial \, h)$. Again it must be that $u(h) = u(n)$. Since we want to avoid this constraint (and Principles 8 and 9 can't be spared), we have to drop Principle 2.

This may begin to look serious. Principle 2 is closely related to our basic Principle 1: the two are equivalent, given Principle 3, that of consequentialism. That is, given

$$u(h \, \partial \, k) = u(o_{h,k}) \quad \text{and} \tag{3}$$
$$u(h \, \partial \, m) = u(o_{h,m}),$$

(2) is equivalent to

$$u(h) = p(k,h)u(o_{h,k}) + p(m,h)u(o_{h,m}). \tag{1}$$

But (1) has already been qualified (in the preceding section). We held that a person governs his actions in the light of how he now sees things. Where he starts out undecided, what he comes to want reflects the utilities of the propositions reporting the outcomes *as he understands them*. The outcome-reporting propositions in (1) are $o_{h,k}$ and $o_{h,m}$. We will say that (1) applies only where $o_{h,k}$ *and* $o_{h,m}$ *report the outcomes as they are understood by the agent.*

Let us put it in fewer words; a new special term will help. A proposition reporting a fact the way the agent understands that fact will be described as *compelling* for that agent (we might have called it *salient*). This allows us to compress the proviso just attached to (1). In its short form, the proviso says that *both $o_{h,k}$ and $o_{h,m}$ are compelling*. Principle 1 will hold for us only with that proviso attached, and the same proviso also will be attached to Principle 3.

Should we relax our other principles along these lines too? We might attach to (10) the proviso that *h-and-k* is compelling and to (2) the proviso that *h-and-k* and *h-and-m* are compelling. But this would often require our setting the same utility on h as on *h-and-k* even where, though we think k is true, k is no part of our understanding of what h reports. This restriction we do not need; indeed, it is one we are well off without.[26] So we had better avoid it.

Let us instead make use of the idea of *conditional* understandings, the idea of a person's dispositions to understand things if he believed, say, *k*. Building on that, we will add two concepts. We will say *h* is *k-preemptive* for someone where *h* would be (or would remain) compelling for him if he believed *k*, that is, where *h* would then report what it reports the way he understood it. We will say *h* is *k-adoptive* for him where it isn't *k*-preemptive and, moreover, if he believed *k*, he would understand the fact *h* reports as the conjunction *h-and-k*. Loosely put, *h* is *k*-adoptive for a person where, if he now believed *k*, *k* would contribute to how he sees what is reported by *h*.

To focus this, suppose that someone is ill. He may just see that as *I am ill;* if so, *I am ill* is compelling for him. If he now learned that his friend won the lottery, he would of course be glad, but very likely that would not enter his understanding of his own situation. *I am ill* is likely to be *my-friend-won-the-lottery*-preemptive for him. But suppose that things would change if he learned that some drug would soon cure him. That is, suppose he wouldn't then see his situation as *I am ill* but as *I am ill and about to get better.* Here *I am ill* is *I-am-about-to-get-better*-adoptive for this person.

Back now to Principle 2; the trouble that causes is easily fixed. We will attach this proviso to (2), that *h is both k-adoptive and m-adoptive.* We must now further qualify (3), adding the same proviso that *h is k-adoptive and m-adoptive* to the earlier proviso about the outcome propositions being compelling. A similar proviso reinstates (10), the proviso that *h is k-adoptive.* The adoptiveness provisos are being attached to principles that present the utility of *h* or of certain of its outcome reports in terms of the utility of that proposition conjoined with one or more

---

26 We will see why in Chapter 4. The point is made more directly in my "Allowing for Understandings," forthcoming.

others. They confine the force of these principles to where that (or those) other proposition(s), if believed, would contribute to the agent's understanding of what is reported by h.

The qualified (10) and (2) don't impose the constraint we saw that we had to avoid, that a person must set the same utility on propositions he thinks coreportive. Suppose again that the agent believes that h and n are coreportive. The new (10) and (2) here get us $u(h) = u(n)$ only in special cases, only where h is (h-*iff-n*)-adoptive and n is (n-*iff-h*)-adoptive. They get us $u(h) = u(n)$ only where what is reported by h is understood by the agent as *h-and-*(h-*iff-n*) and what is reported by n is understood as *n-and-*(n-*iff-h*). The doctor who set different utilities on *my patient will recover* and *that murderer will recover* saw the fact these propositions report in one of these two ways. So he did not also see it as any conjunctive compound of them (this by univocity), and our new provisoed principles cannot fault his valuations.

Some readers may want an expectedness principle less saddled with provisos than (1) or (2). If so, they might now recall

$$u(h) = p(k,h)u(h,k) + p(m,h)u(h,m), \qquad (11)$$

which holds given only that $p(k\text{-}\mathscr{C}\text{-}m, h) = 0$. Nothing excessive follows from (11). Where we think h and n coreportive, we get just $u(h) = u(h, h\text{-}iff\text{-}n)$ and $u(n) = u(n, n\text{-}iff\text{-}h)$, and so we don't need to cut back (11) to avoid getting $u(h) = u(n)$. In Chapter 2, given (10) as it was, (11) and (2) were equivalent, but (11) is now the more general principle: it holds where (2) does not. Where h is k-adoptive and m-adoptive, (11) reduces to (2) *via* (10). Where it isn't, (2) does not apply but (11) does apply. Notice that, to square (11) with (1), it has to be that

$$u(h,k) = u(o_{h,k}) \quad \text{and} \qquad (12)$$
$$u(h,m) = u(o_{h,m}),$$

though only where $o_{h,k}$ and $o_{h,m}$ are compelling.

We can finally return to our troublesome principle of closure. We can bring back that principle, too, with a proviso attached.

A Missing Factor

Let us put it this way, that if a person wants *h* and believes *k*, and if *m* follows from *h-and-k* . . . , *and if both h and m are compelling*, then this person also wants *m*. The modified principle is weaker than the original. It doesn't imply that if someone believes that *h* and *m* are coreportive and wants one of them, he also wants the other, and this was the implication that raised the problem we noted. For Orwell, *h: I shoot that fellow human* was compelling and *m: I shoot that Fascist* was not. For the Frenchman, neither *h: I join the war* nor *m: I leave my mother* was compelling. So they remain in the clear.

Let us get some perspective on our various modifications. We have attached certain special provisos, but this itself is no novelty. Several of the principles with which we started come with provisos already attached. Both our initial (1) and (2) hold only where $p(k-\&-m,h) = 0$, and (6) holds only where, if the agent believed *k*, he would believe *not-both-h-and-m*. The new departure here is not the attachment of provisos to principles; it is the attachment of provisos that allow for the agent's understandings. Our modified principles all refer to how the agent understands certain facts or to certain conditional understandings. Thus these principles (and the principle of univocity) bring understandings into the logic of coherence.

A Technical Note. The reader may be uneasy with our new provisos on formal grounds. He may suspect that the unprovisoed principles, or some of them, follow from more basic theses, from certain theses about coherent preferences. There is a pertinent existence theorem first established by Ethan Bolker and advanced also by Richard Jeffrey.[27] From certain conditions on a

---

27 See Ethan D. Bolker, "A Simultaneous Axiomatization of Utility and Subjective Probability," *Philosophy of Science* 34 (1967); the proof itself appears in Bolker's "Functions Resembling Quotients of Measures," *Transactions of the American Mathematical Society* 124 (1966). See also Richard C. Jeffrey, *The Logic of Decision*, 2nd ed. (Chicago: University of Chicago Press, 1983), Chap. 9 (first edition in 1965).

person's preferences one can deduce the existence of utilities and probabilities that reflect the preferences he has, but only if these utilities and probabilities satisfy the unprovisoed (2).

I find no problem with the existence theorem because I reject the Bolker-Jeffrey conditions on preference. In particular, I reject the condition they call *impartiality*. Let us say *h* is *indifferent* to *k* where neither is preferred to the other. Impartiality requires that, where *h* is indifferent to *k*, if *h* implies *not-k* and *k* implies *not-h* and both relate likewise (that is, by exclusion) to some *m* that is *not* indifferent to *h*, then if *h-or-m* is indifferent to *k-or-m* for that *m*, *h-or-m* is indifferent to *k-or-m* for every such *m*.

If we accept the usual theory, this of course must hold. But what if we don't accept that theory? Bolker and Jeffrey both concede that impartiality has no independent credentials. The only case for it begs the question. Jeffrey is perfectly candid: "The axiom [of impartiality] is there because we need it, and it is justified by our antecedent belief in the plausibility of the result we mean to deduce from it."[28] We won't be needing the axiom in this book. We do not "mean to deduce" results from it; indeed, we want to deny precisely what Jeffrey wants to deduce (the unprovisoed (2)). So we are free to reject it. And if we reject impartiality, the existence theorem has no force against us.

3.8 INTENSIONALITY

Our theory attends to how the agent understands certain facts. It makes allowance for his understandings by lifting constraints the usual theory imposes. Let us consider the sorts of constraints and liftings that are involved.

We will need some new technical terms. Theories of the kind that we have refer to mental states or attitudes. We will speak of the level of the *intensionality* (with an "*s*") of such theories and

28 Jeffrey, *The Logic of Decision*, p. 147. See also Bolker, "A Simultaneous Axiomatization . . . ," pp. 337–8.

attitudes, and also of its converse, of their level of *extensionality*. This we will take to express, on one hand, the extent to which the theories are logically unconstraining, and on the other, what the theories say about the attitudes that they study. Starting now with attitudes, we will distinguish three levels.

Let $A(\cdot)$ be any attitude type, any *propositional* attitude type (e.g., belief, or desire, or the utility valuation x). Let $A(h)$ and $A(k)$ be particular attitudes, instances of $A(\cdot)$ (e.g., a belief that h). Let $jA(h)$ say that someone, j, has attitude A toward h (e.g., that Jack believes h). Let "$\rightarrow$" be short for "implies." $A(\cdot)$ is *weakly* intensional where it isn't true of every j, h, and k that

$$h\text{-}iff\text{-}k \rightarrow jA(h)\text{-}iff\text{-}jA(k).$$

$A(\cdot)$ is weakly intensional where it doesn't follow from h and k's being materially equivalent that if any j has A toward h, j also has A toward k and *vice versa*. This is a concept of no special interest. All attitude types are weakly intensional; no question has ever been raised about that. I bring in the concept for contrast with the others and because it echoes the familiar idea of *propositional* intensionality, the idea of the non-truthfunctionality of certain compound propositions.

The questions have to do with the other two levels. $A(\cdot)$ is *strictly* intensional where it isn't true of every j, h, and k that

$$h \text{ and } k \text{ are coreportive} \rightarrow jA(h)\text{-}iff\text{-}jA(k).$$

$A(\cdot)$ is *strongly* intensional where it isn't true of every j, h, and k that

$$h \text{ and } k \text{ are coreportive and } j \text{ believes this} \rightarrow jA(h)\text{-}iff\text{-}jA(k).$$

Where $A(\cdot)$ is intensional to any degree, we will say that its instances are too. And we will say that the negations of weak, strict, and strong intensionality are strong, strict, and weak *ex*tensionality, in that order. Notice that strong intensionality implies strict intensionality and that strict intensionality implies weak intensionality. (The implications for extensionality go the same way: strong extensionality implies strict extensionality, which implies weak extensionality.)

This is for the special case of attitudes focusing on single propositions only, but it is easily generalized for cases involving multiple foci. We need just to extend the antecedents of our formulas to have them apply to *n* pairs of propositions (any *n*, not just 1, as above). Take, for instance, the supposition of the strong intensionality of conditional utilities. This says that it doesn't follow from the fact that *h* and *h'* are coreportive and that *k* and *k'* are too and that, moreover, some *j* believes this that, for *j*, $u(h,k) = x$ iff $u(h',k') = x$. The amplification for $n = 2$ of our formula for strong intensionality will cover this thesis.

Intensionality, as we define it, has to do with what implies what, and so it has us look to what our theories say on that. Every theory lets every $A(\cdot)$ be weakly intensional: no theory requires of any $A(\cdot)$ that, for every *j*, *h*, and *k*, if *h-iff-k*, then *jA(h)-iff-jA(k)*. In other respects, some theories of mind (of mental states) are more constraining than others. We saw in Section 3.7 that the usual theory constrains the equivalence of certain ascriptions of desires (as in Orwell's and the Frenchman's cases) and of utilities (the doctor's case). It makes these attitudes weakly extensional – it keeps them at most *strictly intensional*. Our revised theory doesn't impose these constraints; more precisely, our provisos lift them.

Suppose that a theory is unconstraining to a certain extent, that it does not constrain the equivalence of any ascriptions of certain attitudes. The theory then specifies a certain level of intensionality for these attitudes, and it can itself be said to be intensional up to that level. Our own theory provides for someone's believing *h* and not believing a coreportive *k* (where he doesn't think them coreportive). So it takes beliefs to be strictly (but not strongly) intensional, and it can itself be said to be strictly intensional too. The theory also provides for *wanting h* and not wanting a coreportive *k* where the two are thought coreportive, and so it takes desires to be *strongly* intensional. Thus the theory itself can also be said to be strongly intensional.

Again, all attitudes are weakly intensional; no questions come up on that score. The questions are about the higher levels, about whether any are strictly intensional and whether any are intensional *strongly* (whether all attitudes are strictly extensional, and whether all are extensional weakly). Are desires and utilities strongly intensional, as our theory holds? This comes down to whether that theory should be as unconstraining as we have made it, as profusely provisoed. Our answer is of course *yes*, this because, as we will soon see, the theory explains what a more constraining one can't. Are beliefs and probabilities strongly intensional too? Should the theory be *less* constraining? Our answer is *no*, because we don't need it less constraining.

We sometimes don't need it as lax as we made it, that is, with all the provisos we added. The new provisos allow for under-standings, but we can sometimes explain people's actions with-out taking note of their understandings. The assumption then is that, in these cases, their understandings don't make any differ-ence, that people would act the same in these cases however they saw their options and the rest. Where that is true, the usual theory (without the provisos) works well enough.

Here is the economist Kenneth Arrow, reflecting on his sub-ject: "A fundamental concept of rationality, so elementary that we hardly notice it, is . . . its *extensionality.* "[29] He brings up the logic of budget sets. A budget set is an opportunity set, and this can be taken to be a set of propositions reporting different con-sumption patterns, a set from which the agent wants (and can afford) to select just one. Say that the items in sets S and S' are pairwise coreportive. Whoever has this information faces one consumption issue if he faces the other. Also, if s is an item of S and s' is the matched item in S', the agent who knows they are

---

29 "Risk Perception in Psychology and Economics," *Economic Inquiry* 20 (1982), p. 6.

coreportive wants (or will come to want) *s* if and only if he wants (or will want) *s'*. Arrow calls this an "axiom," and he would doubtless generalize: in any proper economic context, if *h* and *k* are coreportive and the agent knows it, if he wants one, he wants the other. He is saying that, for economics, people's desires are (at most) strictly intensional – that they are (at least) weakly *ex*tensional.

Where the theory of certain behavior imposes an extensionality constraint, we can take that as saying something about the logic applicable there. It may be that our initial logic, without the provisos, can be used in those contexts, that Arrow's axiom or something like it is true of both desires and utilities there. I find no problem with the idea of logics of different strengths holding in different contexts. The special logic of microeconomics is simpler and stronger than our general logic. It is more constraining, but its constraints sometimes fit the facts. The refinements proposed above in this chapter don't demand any break with what works. They don't imply that the usual logic, without the provisos, must be left behind but only that in many cases we can't depend much on it.

Let me note a sort of extensionality we haven't yet mentioned, call it *logical* extensionality. *A* (•) is logically *ex*tensional where it *is* true of every *j, h,* and *k* that

h and k are logically equivalent → *jA*(*h*)*-iff-jA*(*k*).

To this constraint we are clearly committed. The principle of substitutivity (in Section 2.8) imposes it on all the basic attitudes, on beliefs and desires and on probabilities and utilities. So the logical extensionality of these attitudes only recalls us to substitutivity.

Suppose that you are sick and considering a risky medical treatment. One doctor tells you that the treatment will give you a 60% chance of surviving the year and an 80% chance of surviving five. A second doctor warns you, however, that if you have the treatment, you will have a 40% chance of *dying* within the year and a 20% chance of dying within five. You want the prospect the first doctor offers and don't want the prospect of which the second doctor warns.[30] Yet the two prospects are logically equivalent. Does your thinking violate substitutivity?

Or ask yourself whether the utility you set on having half your life behind you is the same as that which you set on having half your life still ahead. *My life is half over* and *half my life is ahead* are logically equivalent propositions. Yet many people set a higher utility on the latter than on the former, or so what they say suggests. Again, does this violate substitutivity?

Yes it does, but no need to panic. Recall that our principles are idealizations, that they are idealizations of the Aristotelian sort (see Section 2.9). They abstract from causal factors whose effects are unpredictable for us, from distraction and drowsiness and distress. These are a kind of psychic drag; we know we must make some allowance for them and we know at least roughly how. For instance, take lack of logical acuity. Where a person does not notice the logical equivalence of certain propositions, substitutivity may well fail – hence the medical-prospects story. Or consider a person's anxiety when he reflects on his aging. This may lead to lapses too, as in the valuation of half his life being over.

So we can keep the substitutivity principle and logical exten-sionality (which is consequent from it). But if this line of think-ing is open, why didn't we take it throughout? We noted that Orwell and Sartre's young Frenchman violated closure as that is usually put. Why didn't we simply say at that point that every idealization sometimes falls short, that closure is no exception? Why didn't we account for how they were thinking by pointing to background frictional factors (emotional tension perhaps)? Our principles could then have stayed as they were, without the provisos we added. The answer is that we wanted a theory that was more self-contained. Blaming the failures of a theory we

---

30 You are not alone in this; see Arrow, ibid., p. 7.

have on exogenous factors is passing the buck. It leaves us open to the challenge that we have turned our backs on the problems. If that is our answer, can we stop where we are? We have brought understandings in. Should we be resting content with that? The *mentalizing* idea (in Section 2.9) shows how we might take in logical acuity, how we might provide for the cases in which a person is lacking in it, and we could doubtless add further refinements. With the theory then more comprehensive, more of the buck would stop with us.

Still, that wouldn't be all to the good. Leaving some factors out can make sense, for bringing them in isn't free. The more we build into our theory, the more we need to consider. The richer the theory, the harder it is to apply. We face a trade-off here: either more inclusion or greater ease of application. I have traded-off one way. The reader may trade-off differently.

4

SOME APPLICATIONS

MANY philosophers have written about it, recently more than ever before. Conflict remains a fact of life, all these studies notwithstanding. A person is often "divided" on some issue, often is prompted in opposite ways. How can someone be in a conflict with himself alone, and how can he get himself out of it? Also, how serious is it for him if he doesn't get out?

A person in a conflict wants two propositions he knows can't both hold. He wants h and also k and believes that if h then *not-k*, and thus that if k then *not-h*. This concept is comprehensive. It covers deep conflicts and trivial ones, moral conflicts and nonmoral ones. If h and k are both morally urgent, you are involved in a moral conflict. But say that you want to move to Utah and also to move to Maine; this conflict is morally neutral.

Some thinkers do not accept the idea of a person's having incompatible desires. How can a person knowingly want what would defeat his own wants? Plato tells a story about

> ... Leontion, the son of Aglaion, who was on his way up from the Peiraeus, under the outer side of the north wall, when he noticed some corpses lying on the ground with the executioner standing by them. He wanted to go and look at them, and yet at the same time held himself back in disgust. For a time he struggled with himself and covered his eyes, but at last his desire got the better of him and he ran up to the corpses, opening his eyes wide and saying to them, "There you are, curse you – a lovely sight! Have a real good look!"[1]

1 Plato, *Republic*, 439e.

102

This story smacks of a paradox for him. What sense does it make to argue with oneself?

Plato finds an answer that suits him in the analogy of conflicts between people. He takes the metaphor of a "divided self" literally. There are, for him, three selves in each soul, each of them capable of beliefs and desires. The sorts of beliefs and desires each has are distinctive of that sort of self, and the desires of any part-self can conflict with those of any other. For Leontion it came to this, that one part of him wanted one thing and another part wanted the opposite. The inner conflict disturbing his psyche was an outer conflict of two of its parts.

This is certainly vivid. And let us suppose we allow for this picture, that we allow for beliefs and desires not being states of whole unitary *persons*. Still, why should we think it correct? Why believe that, strictly speaking, a unit psyche can't be in conflict, that what looks like self-opposition calls for a split-soul analysis? I can find no good answers to this. Plato says that "one and the same thing cannot act or be affected in opposite ways at the same time in the same part of it and in relation to the same object . . . ."[2] But here the opposite reactions (wanting and not-wanting) are to *h* and to *not-k* (to *I look at those corpses* and *I yield to temptation*), and these two are not "the same object."

Was Plato troubled by the idea of someone's being in a contradiction? Or better, ought we today to be troubled? Should the following *reductio* give us pause? A person in conflict with himself wants both *h* and *k* and thinks that each rules out the other. Since he wants *h* and believes *if-h-then-not-k*, closure implies that he also wants *not-k*. But then he wants both *k* and *not-k* and so is in a contradiction. By closure again, he wants *k-and-not-k* too, and from this everything follows. So he wants *m*, whatever *m* might be. There isn't any such all-wanting person. No one is therefore in conflict with himself.

2 Ibid., 436b.

This argument rests on that principle of closure to which, in the last chapter, we attached a proviso. When we have that proviso in place, the argument breaks down. The provisoed principle implies that if a person wants *h* and believes *if-h-then-not-k* . . . , *and if both h and not-k are compelling,* he then also wants *not-k.* In many cases of conflict, this proviso isn't met. Where it is not (think of the Frenchman), the agent's conflict does not yield a contradiction: he isn't bound by logic to want *k* and also to want *not-k.* So he isn't stuck with wanting *k-and-not-k* and all that follows from that.

A person in conflict who meets the proviso is of course in a bind. Logic requires such a person to want much more than he does, and he is likely to handle this problem by letting logic go hang. He will not bother with closure. This last needn't make us uneasy, for, on our theory, the theses of logic are idealizations only. They say what people would be like if there were no disturbing factors. One such factor is prurience, which Leontion couldn't resist: a person seized by unwelcome lusts may very well be inconsistent. He is not likely to satisfy closure, with or without the provisos, and it cannot affect our theory when in fact he doesn't.

Why then should one have any doubt that there are conflicts in the same psyche? In default of an answer to this, we will put all doubts aside. Things are here just what they seem. Leontion wanted one thing and he also wanted the opposite. So also, often, do each of the rest of us, more often perhaps than we think. There is no problem in this.

4.2 SETTLING IT

The problem of conflict is different: it is what to do when you find yourself in one. A simple solution is to get yourself out. Your wanting *h* and an incompatible *k* isn't contradictory but it can be troubling. Since you can't act both on *h* and on *k,* which way ought you to turn? If you stopped wanting one or the other, you would be in the clear. The question this raises is how to retrench, and the usual answer is *inquiry*. Take the trouble to learn what you can. Consult with others, read all the books, get to know all the facts of the case. When you do, your conflict will lift – you will have come to resolve it.

This has the ring of common sense, and it is sometimes the natural course. You want to move to Utah and also to move to Maine. Learn some more about those places. Lots of Mormons in Utah: a very conservative state. Not a state in which one does the sorts of things you do. Let that simmer in your mind and Utah may look less attractive to you. You may no longer want to live there. That would resolve your conflict.

Sometimes indeed, the more you know, the less you continue to want, and, again, such unloading may help. But often your wants are not affected. You then remain in conflict. Is an inquiry bound to work if it is pressed far enough? We can let this question go, for there is a second way out. This second way is more common than inquiry, though little attention is paid to it. I will call it *persuasion*. Let us now briefly consider that.

Here, for a start, is a two-person conflict and some (attempted) bilateral persuasion. In 1976, the Supreme Court decided the case of *Gregg v. Georgia*, which had to do with the death penalty. The majority of the justices held that the Constitution can't be said to exclude it. Justice Stewart, reporting this judgment, wrote that "the death penalty is not a form of punishment that may never be imposed. . . . [W]e cannot say that the punishment is invariably disproportionate to the crime. It is an extreme sanction, suitable to the most extreme of crimes."[3] Justice Brennan, in his dissent, wrote that a state execution "involves, by its very nature, a denial of the executed person's humanity. . . . [I]t treats members of the human race as nonhumans, as objects to be toyed with and discarded. It is thus inconsistent with the fundamental premise of the Clause [disallowing cruel and

3 *United States Reports* 428, p. 187.

unusual punishments] that even the vilest criminal remains a human being possessed of common human dignity."[4]

Stewart and Brennan doubtless tried to persuade each other before they voted. What were they then doing? Neither was offering any information he thought the other did not have – neither was making a contribution to any *inquiry* on the other's part. Nor need it be that either was trying to change what the other wanted, to shake that other loose from how he wanted the case (as he saw it) to go. Both of them were rewriting the case. They were reshaping the issue on which the Court would have to vote.

The issue, neutrally put, was this: States shall be free to execute certain of their convicted felons / they shall *not* be free to do this. Justice Stewart put it this way instead: States shall be free to impose extreme sanctions / they shall *not* be free to do this. Justice Brennan tried to make it this: States shall be free to deny a convict his basic human dignity / they shall *not* be free to do it. We can here speak of three different issues, though of course they are closely related. Their different first options pick out the same course, and so do their second options. Killing certain convicts is the same as imposing an extreme sanction and also the same as denying them a minimal human dignity, and under the circumstances, *not* killing these people is the same as *not* imposing such a sanction and the same too as *not* denying them dignity. The issues differ in this, that each lays out the two courses differently, that is, as different propositions.

Why would anyone bother to promote one of these issues over the other? Why would he try to turn our minds from *these* propositions to *those*, to try to persuade us to think in their terms? Because he knows that our thinking that way would connect with desires we had all along, desires that echo his own. Changing the issue is changing the subject, and on the subject he is bringing up for us, this person knows we agree with him.

Settling It

Stewart knew that Brennan wanted adequate sanctions imposed against crime. Brennan knew that Stewart wanted even a convict's humanity valued. By getting the other to see things as he did, each hoped to enlist the other's support.

This rests on our thesis about the objects of wanting, that they are not any facts in the raw but the facts reported somehow, that what a person wants is always that some proposition be true. A person may want a proposition h and not want a coreportive proposition k, and this even where he knows that the two propositions are coreportive. It also relates to our thesis on action, that a desire for h may be dormant. That is, it may be ineffective, h not expressing the way the agent understands any fact. To succeed in persuading another is to shape (or *re*shape) his understandings so as to stir up desires in him that had been dormant before. It is to get him to see certain facts so that the desires evoked then move him, to see things somehow that gives him a reason to act as he wouldn't have otherwise.

So much for someone's persuading another. What now of one-person cases? How does a person persuade *himself?* We are assuming that he is conflicted, that he wants h and also wants k and knows it can't be both. Say that he sees no option as either an h'ing or a k'ing. This means that he lacks a full reason for acting either way (he lacks the requisite understandings) and that his partial reasons diverge (he wants both h and k). With the completion of this or that reason, the problem he has will lift. Persuasion completes a reason for him by adding a suitable understanding. Whether he reaches that understanding on his own or is prompted by someone else makes no difference.

Persuasion can work another way too. A person who wants h and an incompatible k may come to see some option as an h'ing, which may then lead him to cease to want k. Here the final effect is retrenchment, the same as that of an inquiry. Perhaps if the Frenchman had come to see his joining the army in those terms – as his *joining the army* – he would have ceased to also want to stay at home with his mother. His new understanding would have worked indirectly, by changing the desires he had. Our theory allows for such self-persuasion, but it allows too for the sort we are noting, in which the new understanding plays an independent role.

A different example may help. Take the case of Rubashov in Koestler's novel *Darkness at Noon*. The accusation against him is false. Rubashov insists he is innocent. The public examiner dismisses this plea. The issue is closed; the verdict will be *guilty*. The truth does not matter, the examiner says, for that verdict will serve the cause. He argues that a confession would do even better. It would be a public sensation. It would shock people into a sense of the danger the Party is in. Rubashov is an Old Bolshevik and has made the Party his life. Nothing else should now enter his mind.

In this we still have one of two people trying to persuade the other. But imagine Rubashov in his cell, debating it with himself. He wants to serve the Party but also wants to keep his good name. The more he thinks about what he might do, the less his reputation figures in it. He knows his public regard is at stake, but he can't keep that in focus. He comes to see the issue as either serving the Party or not, and that puts an end to his conflict. Since he had wanted all along to serve, his course is now fully clear to him.

Let us here notice an ambiguity in the *ending* of conflicts. Conflicts might be *resolved*. In such a case, the agent retrenches; he ceases to want either *h* or *k*. This happens where inquiry sours him on one or the other of them, and also in a persuasion in which he cuts back what he wants. Not so, of course, with Rubashov, who wanted at the end what he had wanted all along. In that sense, he stayed conflicted: his conflict remained unresolved. And yet too, his conflict was over – he now knew what to do. With one of his options (under a certain description) compelling for him, his conflict was *settled*.

Conflicts may be unresolved and yet be settled and so not troubling, and sometimes they are settled from the start. The agent then wants both *h* and *k* and believes that if *h* then *not-*

108

k, but, from the start, either *h* or *k*, one or the other, was compelling for him. We may all have many such quiet, long-established unresolved conflicts. But whether recent or long-established, a conflict that is settled is not a predicament. A settled conflict remains a conflict, but it doesn't block action.[5]

Here is another *un*quiet case, again a self-persuasion. An army officer is assigned to a project he thinks will turn out being brutal. He wants to get himself out of the job but also to follow orders. He reminds himself that he is a junior officer and that it isn't his job to decide. He recalls the oath that he took. He reflects on the meaning of discipline. Thinking this way, he brings himself over. His objections slip out of focus and he accepts the assignment. His conflict remains – it isn't resolved. But it has been settled.

A glimpse ahead: was the officer right? Should he have focused his mind as he did? Ought a person to see brutality as just following orders? What about Rubashov too? Should he have seen his confession as a service? He did in fact serve the cause by lying; still, was he thinking properly there or was he just being had? And what about the judges whom Stewart and Brennan persuaded? Could they all (on both sides) have been right? The answers we get in these cases may differ, but the question is the same each time. When is an understanding of a situation *proper?* Suppose a report of the facts is correct – when is it (what makes it) *appropriate?* When is a person representing things rightly, and when is he *mis*representing them?

Persuasion can sometimes lead someone wrong. It can mislead where it is self-addressed no less than where it is addressed to another. When does it mislead and when doesn't it, or again, when are we seeing things right? I will put this question off. (It is the topic of Chapter 5.)[6]

5 That unresolved conflicts needn't block action is stressed by Isaac Levi in his *Hard Choices* (Cambridge University Press, 1986), esp. Chap. 2.
6 For more about inquiry and persuasion and the like, see my "Coping With Conflict," *Journal of Philosophy* 85 (1988).

4.3 WEAKNESS OF WILL

Suppose that a person wants h and also k, thinking them incompatible, and that he wants h *more* than k (that the utility he sets on h is greater than that which he sets on k). He thinks he might now bring about either, yet he moves to establish k. How is such a thing possible? How can someone seek what he thinks is the lesser of two goods he thinks he might have? This is the problem of weakness of will.

The skeptic offers to save us some trouble. He dismisses the problem: there is no weakness of will. A person is sometimes held back by force and made to compromise somehow, but on his own he always goes for what he himself wants most. No doubt it often looks otherwise, but appearances often deceive.

Take a former heavy smoker, just a month free of the habit. He has sworn to give it up; he is convinced that his life is at stake. But the man at the next table is smoking, and his nostrils fill with desire. Sheepishly, he lights up again. The skeptic argues: what does this prove? Not that this person's will was weak, that a lesser desire won out. His acting on the desire to smoke proves that that was the greater desire.

Or take Leontion after his fall, gaping at the corpses. He had dropped in his own estimation, having failed his ideals. His lusts had been too insistent; he wanted that day to feast his eyes more than he wanted to stay high-minded. Thus again, no weakness of will.

It may be that the skeptic is right about these particular cases. Still, must every story like them yield to his sort of analysis? He argues that people's strengths of desire can be inferred from how they act, that their actions *reveal* their preferences, for what they want most intensely to do determines the action they take. He says, "You asked how someone can seek the lesser of two goods he thinks he might have. The answer is that he can't. Given that he thinks he might have either (and cannot have both) and reaches for one of them, he must want that one more. If in fact he preferred the other, he would have moved for that other. This follows from the usual theory of action."

Yes, but it doesn't follow from ours, for in our theory we take account also of the understandings the agent has. Let us recast that theory slightly, putting it here not in terms of *wanting* but in terms of *wanting more than*. Where someone wants *h* more than *k*, and he believes he could bring about either and must bring about one or the other, *and he sees some course he might take as a bringing about of h*, he now brings about *h*. So, on our theory, weakness is possible. That is, our theory (unlike the usual) allows for a person's being weak: it allows for his seeking the lesser of two goods he thinks he might have. He might go for that lesser good if he sees no option he has as his getting the greater. Say he wants *h* more than *k;* where he sees some option as a *k*'ing and sees none as an *h*'ing, he might go for *k*.

Think of the former smoker. He wants to avoid risking his life more than he wants to smoke yet again. But he moves for the lesser good, the tobacco aroma having so enticed him that he can't think of avoiding risk. The smoker's avoiding risk is *h* and his smoking is *k*, and he sees some option as a *k*'ing and sees no option as an *h*'ing. Likewise too with Leontion. He wants to stay high-minded more than he wants to gape. But he sees one option as a gaping and can't focus now on high-mindedness.

Perhaps I have the facts here wrong. Perhaps what happened instead was simply that these people's desires had changed, that the smoker, distracted by smoke, came to prefer his smoking to not smoking and that Leontion came to prefer his gaping to not gaping. If that is what happened, there was no weakness: they both went for what they most wanted. My point is not that smokers are weak, nor indeed that anyone is, that weakness of will must be admitted (though I don't doubt that it must). My point is only that weakness is possible and that we can make good sense of it, that the new theory of action we have makes due allowance for it.

A weakness of the agent's will reveals an incompleteness of some reason for acting. The will (desire) component of that reason is left ineffective by the lack of an understanding. Let us go back to Aristotle, who had the idea first. Or rather, since what he says on the subject is put only very obscurely, let us go to a paraphrase by Wiggins of a central passage in the *Ethics*. Wiggins has Aristotle saying this:

> ... [W]hen there is some major premise or other [which combines with some minor premise to] constrain the man from eating of something ... and when there is another practical syllogism [practical reasoning] in the offing with the major premise that everything sweet is nice to eat and a minor premise that *x* is sweet ... and appetite backs this syllogism; then the former syllogism forbids the man to taste but appetite's syllogism pushes him on. So it turns out that a man behaves incontinently. ... Since the second premise (the minor) is a judgment deriving from perception and is the hinge on which all action must turn, it is of this premise that the incontinent man is prevented by his condition from properly possessing himself.[7]

Wiggins holds that this account is "inconsistent with common sense." Either the agent reaches the conclusion of the health-minded reasoning, in which case he should be acting it out, which (being weak) he isn't. Or he does *not* reach that conclusion, in which case there isn't even a conflict, without which there can be no weakness. The last bit is certainly wrong. Suppose that the agent does not reach the conclusion. He remains conflicted by the desires reported in his major premises.

The agent's conflict consists of his wanting to stay in good health and yet also wanting some sweets though he thinks them unhealthy. He wants to stay in good health more than he wants the sweets, and yet he moves for the sweets, this because he "perceives" them as sweets and not as being unhealthy. He

---

7 David Wiggins, "Weakness of Will, Commensurability, and the Objects of Deliberation and Desire," *Proceedings of the Aristotelian Society* 79 (1978/79), pp. 260–1. The original passage is in the *Nichomachean Ethics*, 1147a–b.

doesn't see declining the sweets as the path of good health. Its being that path is the premise of which the agent, though he *knows* it is true, "is prevented by his condition [his need for sugar?] from properly possessing himself." The health-concerned reasoning is not concluded because its minor premise (the "hinge") is missing. And thus it is the absence of this premise, or the lack of the understanding it would have expressed, that accounts for the agent's weakness – his gobbling the sweets. (The case is just like the smoker's: in place of the sweets put the cigarette, etc.)

Still another case may help. Let us look at Huck Finn's conflict. Huck found himself torn between helping his friend and doing the right thing morally. He couldn't do both, or so he believed, for his friend Jim was a runaway slave, and acting rightly meant turning him in. A boy who did wrong faced the fires of hell; of this he had no doubt. And so he made up his mind. The time had come to reform. He wrote a letter to Jim's master and relaxed, and "felt good and washed clean of sin for the first time I ever felt so in my life." But then he

> ... got to thinking over our trip down the river; and I see Jim before me all the time: in the day and in the night-time, some-times moonlight, sometimes storms, and we a-floating along, talking and singing and laughing. But somehow I couldn't seem to strike no places to harden me against him, but only the other kind. I'd see him standing my watch on top of his'n, 'stead of calling me, so I could go on sleeping; and see him how glad he was when I come back out of the fog; and when I come to see him again in the swamp ... and such-like times. ... [After which] I took up [the letter]. ... I studied a minute ... and then says to myself: "All right, then, I'll *go* to hell" – and tore it up ... and never thought no more about reforming.[8]

Huck had yielded to weakness. He wanted most of all to act rightly – to turn in the outlaw – or so he reports. Still, he could

8 Mark Twain, *The Adventures of Huckleberry Finn* (New York: Harper & Row, 1965), pp. 186–7.

not bring himself to it. He couldn't because he didn't see Jim as the outlaw he thought him to be. He saw him only as a friend: "I couldn't seem to strike no places to harden me against him, but only the other kind." So he couldn't see turning Jim in as acting rightly but only as betrayal. Huck's will (like that of the smoker and the others) was weak because of how he saw his options, because he did not see any option as a pursuit of what he most wanted.

There is another line one might take. On that, Huck's weakness had to do with his neglect of his own beliefs – of his total evidence.[9] Huck turned away in the end from what he took to be the plain truth. He neglected (declined, refused) to attend to all that was relevant, setting aside his own conviction of Jim's being an outlaw. The basic word here is "relevant," and what is relevant is a matter of logic: a relevant item *should* be considered, this in some logical sense of *should*. On the logic that I am proposing, only those beliefs are relevant that bear on his situation as the agent understands it. Given Huck's view of sending that letter as a betrayal of a friend, it wasn't relevant that he thought Jim an outlaw. So he cannot be held to be weak for having put that out of his mind.

I hold that Huck was weak willed, and that it was the way he saw the options he had that made for his weakness. This isn't offered as censure. It doesn't imply that he somehow fell short – still, did he fall short or not? From his own point of view, he did, but what about from ours? The answer depends on how we think he *should* have been seeing his options, on whether we think he should have seen them in terms of slaves and masters or of friendship, and here the *should* is not that of logic but of some other sort. The question comes down to an issue we noted when we spoke about being misled. Should Rubashov have seen his confession as a lie or as a service to the Party? Should

9 This is Donald Davidson's approach in "How is Weakness of the Will Possible?" in his *Essays on Actions and Events*.

the officer have seen brutality as only following orders? We put these matters off above and we must put them off here again. The skeptic reenters, unpersuaded. He refuses to call Huck weak. He says, "It can't be weakness just to go against your desires. It isn't weakness to be living in Podunk when you'd rather be living in Paris if you don't think you could move. A person could be said to be weak only if he went against his *reasons*. On the usual theory of reasons, this means that he didn't do what he wanted though he thought that he could. Your broader theory packs more into reasons. On your theory, to go against his reasons, a person must fail to act on his wants when he not only thinks that he could but sees some option as his doing just that. Huck wanted to do the right thing and he thought that he could, for he thought sending that letter was right. But he did not see it that way – he saw it as ratting on a friend. So he had no full reason for acting. On your new theory, as on the old, there can never be weakness, for what is sometimes reported as weakness only brings out that there was no full reason. There was then nothing to go against."

This moves us from weakness of will alone to a more general idea of weakness, the idea of weakness of *reasons*. Let us accept the skeptic's definition: a reason some person has is weak where he goes against that reason, and he himself is weak there too. On this analysis, Huck was not weak, and nor was the smoker, nor was Leontion. Their wills were weak, but their reasons weren't, since each of them acted on the reason he had.

The skeptic goes beyond this. He draws the conclusion that there never is weakness (weakness of reasons), that our theory excludes it. Our theory does indeed exclude it, but the theory is an idealization and we know that it sometimes fails. To say that someone's reasons were weak is just to say that it failed in his case, that he acted in a way our theory can't explain. Having never made the claim that the theory holds in every context, we face no special problem in the fact that in some contexts it doesn't.

4.4 RESOLUTENESS

There is still another way of thinking about people's weakness. In this, the weakness appears over time. The agent decides to act somehow in the future, but when the time comes, he doesn't. He has formed no new beliefs (or new probabilities) that unsettle his choice. Yet he no longer wants to do what he had decided to do, and so he does not do it.

Looking back on the smoker, we might now fit him into this mold, and it may fit Leontion too. On this different construal of them, these two were not weak in the sense just above. That is, they weren't weak willed: they didn't take any option to which they preferred some other. Their preferences (or desires) had changed under pressure – they pursued the ones they now had. Still, they both had made resolutions that they did not keep. Both were tempted and succumbed to temptation. We can say this about them, that they both were *irresolute*. This sort of weakness is common.

Suppose that the agent, planning ahead, knows that he is irresolute. He deplores this weakness of his, for it may defeat his plans. He now therefore tries to outflank it. Consider Ulysses' famous scheme. The course he had set went right by the Sirens. He knew that no one could resist their singing, that if he kept to the course he had set, he would in time be overcome and be wrecked. Still, he itched to hear the Sirens. So he had himself tied to the mast and had the ears of his sailors plugged up. This last kept the sailors from hearing the singing and also from hearing him pleading with them to head for the shore when he *did* hear it. (I assume his desires had changed when he heard the song, that he then wanted to reach for the Sirens even at the cost of his life. If he still wanted most to sail home, as he had done before, but had been so bewitched by the Sirens that he couldn't now focus on that, he would be like our sworn-off smoker overcome by his neighbor's smoking: nothing new for us there.)

116

Resoluteness

A distinction is sometimes made at this point between myopic and sophisticated choice. A *myopic* chooser makes his decision in the light of his present desires, whatever he thinks he may come to want later. The desires he expects to have in the future are for him those of a different self, whose interests are not his concern. He sees no reason for troubling about them. A chooser who is *sophisticated* knows that myopia can be unstable. He knows that he himself, in the future, acting on his new interests then, may undo his present self's plans. So he takes this into account. He guards against that later self; he opts for the best course from among those courses his later self would complete – from the courses he couldn't undo. That may involve now tying his hands (or tying his body to the mast). The captains who had preceded Ulysses had been myopic and had suffered for it. Ulysses was sophisticated and lived to tell the tale.[10]

Sophistication improves on myopia. Edward McClennen has recently argued that a person could do even better. He notes that Ulysses is paying a price for getting what would have been costless for him had he known he would stick to his purpose. Suppose he had made up his mind to sail by and then been resolute when the time came, doing what he had planned to do, against his then-current inclinations. He could in that case have heard the Sirens without the expense of the rope and the earplugs. (If his sailors weren't resolute, too, there would still have been trouble. So think of Ulysses as sailing alone; he buys and installs an automatic pilot and sets a course he can't later change. Had he known he could trust himself, he could have spared himself this.) McClennen holds that *resolute choosing* – choosing in the conviction of standing firm later – is "pragmatically superior" to sophistication. Since he expects to get the

10 The myopia-sophistication distinction was first discussed by R. H. Strotz; see his "Myopia and Inconsistency in Dynamic Utility Maximization," *Review of Economic Studies* 23 (1955/56).

Some Applications

same for less, a resolute-choosing Ulysses does better for himself (*expects* to do better) than the sophisticated Ulysses did.[11] Resoluteness is a certain persistence, a sticking to one's course though one's interests have changed. Suppose that a person had planned to take *k* over *h* at some point in the future, but when the time comes he wants to take *h* – or he then prefers *h* to *k*. If he is resolute, he takes *k* nonetheless, following out his plan. We meet what looks like a problem here. How, on our theory, is such a thing possible? How can a person act in defiance of his own current desires? In the last section, the challenge was that people sometimes are weak. The new challenge is that our theory fails where people are, in a different sense, strong.

Let me flag a nuisance: the different senses of "weak" and "strong" get in each other's way. Suppose that a person is weak in our initial, static sense (weakness of will). He then thinks *h* and *k* incompatible, wants *h* more than *k*, thinks he could bring about *h*, but moves for *k* instead. The very same holds of someone who is *strong* (or firm, or resolute) in the *dynamic* sense (resolution), though this person then moves for *k* because he had earlier decided to do it. Dynamic strength is static weakness and dynamic weakness is static strength. But this can make no trouble for us if we keep the qualifiers in mind.

The structural parity of static weakness and dynamic strength deserves to be stressed. It suggests that the problem of resoluteness is like that of weakness of will, that the problem in both cases is how one can move for the less-wanted of two options. And that in turn suggests that our analysis of weakness applies to resoluteness too. On the usual theory of action, where a person wants *h* more than *k* and thinks he could bring about *h*,

11 Edward F. McClennen, "Dynamic Choice and Rationality," in B. R. Munier (ed.), *Risk, Decision and Rationality* (Dordrecht: Reidel, 1988). For a fuller analysis, see his *Rationality and Dynamic Choice* (Cambridge University Press, 1990). A similar view is held by Jon Elster, who describes sophistication as "imperfectly rational"; see his *Ulysses and the Sirens* (Cambridge University Press, 1979), Chap. 2.

he goes for *h*. Our revision builds in understandings: the agent must also see some action as a bringing about of *h*. Where he lacks that understanding, he might move for *k*. This is how we accounted above for a person's weakness of will.

Likewise now with resoluteness. Again we must attend to how the options are understood. Suppose that Ulysses has made up his mind to turn his back on the Sirens when he hears them. "No need to tie myself down," he says, and he does not do it. (Forget about the other sailors; he is all alone.) Now at last he hears the singing, and he wants to head for the bliss he expects on shore. If that is how he understands this option (in terms of finding bliss), he takes it. He thought he would be resolute, but it turns out he was wrong.

Suppose, however, his understanding is different. Suppose that, even as he is tempted, his project recalls itself to him. He sees his two options in terms of their bearing on the course he has set. These options, neutrally put, are (*A*) to make for the shore and (*B*) to sail straight ahead. His desire is firm and clear: he much prefers his reaching for bliss to staying the course he has set. But in this second version of the story, he sees taking *A* as moving off his course (not as reaching for bliss), and he sees taking *B* as staying that course (not as forfeiting bliss). The way he sees *A* connects with nothing he wants, and the way he sees *B* connects with his wanting to stay on course. And so our theory says he will do this: it says that he will be resolute.

The resolute agent is as eager for bliss as his irresolute cousin, and they both want to stay on course. They differ not in their desires or preferences, nor (as McClennen holds) in their principles of choice, but in their understandings. They differ in the way they see the options they have. One of them sees his options in terms of the bliss that the Sirens offer him, the other in terms of their different relations to the course he has set. McClennen himself remarks on the distinctive understandings of the resolute agent. He says, "For [a resolute] agent, choice points within a decision tree are *continuation* points: he sees his

Some Applications

task (at each such point) as that of continuing to implement the
plan he initially settled upon. . . . "12

Let me put it another way. A resolute agent is indeed acting
against certain current desires, but what he is doing is in full
keeping with certain others he has. He isn't giving past desires
priority over present ones. Rather, he here is activating some
current, backward-attentive desires – different desires from the
ones he would activate were he now being irresolute. It is his
special understandings that activate those desires of his, that get
him to act on these and not others. This fits in well with our
theory, for it is central to our theory that understandings play
this role. So the theory faces no problem in the behavior of the
resolute agent.

Suppose that a person must now choose some multistage plan
or course of conduct and that he knows that certain courses
allow for reneging at some point later. Should he choose from
among those courses in which he would be resolute throughout? *Yes* if he expects to be resolute, and *no* if he doesn't expect
this, in which case he should choose from the courses in which
he would *not* be resolute. A person who thinks that he will be
resolute and chooses accordingly is rational, just as a person
who doubts his resolution and chooses some suitable sophisticated course is rational.

This leaves it an open question whether he *ought* to be resolute – whether he ought to stick to his purpose when the time
comes to act. From the perspective of his present self, it clearly
pays to be resolute later. For if he will be resolute later (and
knows now that he will be resolute), he can now avoid the cost
and trouble of guarding against himself. But from the perspective of that later self, ought he to be resolute then? I have
suggested that he will be resolute if he sees his options a certain
way, in terms of their advancing or defeating his plans. But
ought he to see them that way?

12 *Rationality and Dynamic Choice*, pp. 158–9.

120

We asked such a question about Huck Finn too, and also about Rubashov and the others. Ought Huck to have seen the options he had in terms of slave owning or friendship? We have put questions of that sort aside. (We will return to them later.) We don't need any answers to them to provide for the point being made. That point is not that we ought to be resolute – always, sometimes, or ever. It is that resolute choices and actions can be made to square with our theory, that neither people's weakness of will nor their resoluteness raises problems for us.

4.5 MIGHT HAVE BEENS

We have seen how the idea of understandings bears on some old and familiar topics. We will turn now to more recent matters. These new matters, unlike the earlier, have to do with uncertainty (risk).

Let us begin with this scenario by Maurice Allais.[13] You find yourself facing two issues, each of which gives you two options. In the first issue, if you take your first option, *A*, you will get a million dollars. If you take your second option, *B*, what you will get depends on the color of a ball that will be drawn from an urn. If the ball is red, you will get nothing; if it is white, you will get a million dollars; if it is blue, you will get five million. In the second issue, if you take your first option, *C*, you will get a million dollars if the ball is either red or blue; if it is white, you will get nothing. If you take your second option, *D*, you will get five million dollars if the ball is blue; if it is not, you will get nothing. You know only that there are 100 balls, one of them

13 See his "Le Comportement de l'homme rationnel devant le risque: Critique des postulats et axiomes de l'école américaine," *Econometrica* 21 (1953). See also the more extended version, "The Foundations of a Positive Theory of Choice involving Risk and a Criticism of the Postulates and Axioms of the American School," in Maurice Allais and Ole Hagen (eds.), *Expected Utility Hypotheses and the Allais Paradox* (Dordrecht: Reidel, 1979).

red, 89 white, and 10 blue. We will write "getting x with the probability y" as "x/y." That lets us put these two issues as follows:

Issue 1

A: 1,000,000/1.0 B: 5,000,000/.10
1,000,000/.89
0/.01

Issue 2

C: 1,000,000/.11 D: 5,000,000/.10
0/.89   0/.90

Which options here would you choose? Allais reports his having presented these issues to many people and that the majority chose A over B and also D over C. He notes that if the expected utility of A is greater than that of B, the expected utility of D *can't* be greater than that of C. That of A is greater than that of B if and only if

$$u(1,000,000) > .10u(5,000,000) + \qquad (i)$$
$$.89u(1,000,000) + .01u(0),$$

and so if and only if

$$.11u(1,000,000) > .10u(5,000,000) + .01u(0). \quad (ii)$$

And the expected utility of D is greater than that of C if and only if

$$.10u(5,000,000) + .90u(0) > \qquad (iii)$$
$$.11u(1,000,000) + .89u(0),$$

and so if and only if

$$.10u(5,000,000) + .01u(0) > .11u(1,000,000). \quad (iv)$$

But (ii) and (iv) are contradictory; if one is true, the other is not. So both of the choices the majority made were not expectedness maximizing, or at least so it seems. That is, the majority of the

122

people here were not expectedness maximizers. Allais declares that he isn't one either. He says he too would choose *A* and *D*. A very similar situation was studied by Daniel Kahneman and Amos Tversky.[14] The structure of the issues presented was this:

Issue 3

A: 2,400/1.0	*B:* 2,500/.33
	2,400/.66
	0/.01

Issue 4

C: 2,400/.34	*D:* 2,500/.33
0/.66	0/.67

The majority of the subjects chose *A* over *B* and also *D* over *C*. For both of these choices to be expectedness maximizing, it would have to be that both

$$.34u(2,400) > .33u(2,500) + .01u(0) \quad \text{and} \qquad (v)$$

$$.33u(2,500) + .01u(0) > .34u(2,400). \qquad\qquad (vi)$$

These can't both be true, so the majority did not follow expectedness in both of these issues.

Here is another of Kahneman and Tversky's experiments in the same vein:

Issue 5

A: 3,000/.90	*B:* 6,000/.45
0/.10	0/.55

Issue 6

C: 3,000/.002	*D:* 6,000/.001
0/.998	0/.999

In this, no option offers any outcome with certainty. Again the majority chose *A* over *B* and *D* over *C*, and these choices too can't both be expectedness maximizing.

14 See their "Prospect Theory: An Analysis of Decision Under Risk," *Econometrica* 47 (1979).

Could it be that the people involved had only failed to think clearly, that the experiments only show that people sometimes are careless? If those in the majority had just made mistakes, a bit of coaching would have led them to retract. In fact, when those who later were coached were asked to do it over, most of them stood their ground.[15] So it would miss the point to say that these people had just failed to maximize. They had positively *declined* or *refused* to take the most promising course.

This at least is the usual conclusion. A common analysis is that people are biased toward a certainty of benefit, and even (as in Issue 5) toward a high probability of benefit, that where they have options that offer them this, they discount (devalue) the others. The thesis is that the expected utilities do not settle how people will act, that we need a concept more general than that of expectedness to account for what happens. The weighted averaging of Principle 1 is, on this view, just a special case. Various alternative utility principles have been proposed for taking its place.[16]

There is another approach, however, and Tversky himself remarks on it. He observes that Allais is turning against a certain prescriptive norm, not against the idea that people always maximize their expected utilities – Allais thinks it clear that they don't – but against the idea that they *should*. On a prescriptive reading of it, the expectedness principle rules out one's choosing both *A* and *D* of Issues 1 and 2, and Allais rejects that ruling. *A* offers the agent the certainty of $1,000,000 while *B* involves a risk. Why not here play it safe with *A*? Since nothing can be had for certain in Issue 2, there is no safe course in that. Why not therefore try for the $5,000,000 – why not here choose *D*?

Tversky admits the plausibility of this case for choosing *A* plus *D*, but he notes that the norm might yet stand. The norm rules

15 This is reported by many observers. See, for instance, Paul Slovic and Amos Tversky, "Who Accepts Savage's Axiom?" *Behavioral Science* 9 (1975).
16 Some of these are noted in Mark J. Machina, "Choices Under Uncertainty: Problems Solved and Unsolved," *Economic Perspectives* 1 (1987).

out this choice pair only if a certain supposition is added, only if we suppose that the choosers see the outcomes as these are laid out above. We must suppose that they see the outcomes solely in terms of the amounts of money to be had. And it may be they don't see them that way.

For a person who sees the outcomes in money terms only, Allais is right: choices of A and D can't both be expectedness maximizing. But what if the chooser sees things differently? What if he sees the zero-money outcome of Allais' option B as *getting nothing when I was sure to get a million if I took option A* or as *getting nothing and kicking myself for choosing as I did?* For a person who sees the outcomes in a way that takes in what might have been – what *would* have been, had he been prudent – the choice of both A and D may well be expectedness maximizing. So also for someone who sees the outcomes in terms of the regret (or relief) they would yield him. It could be argued that such a person should choose A and D on expectedness grounds, and nothing worrisome therefore follows from the fact that many people did.[17]

We can drop the talk of *shoulds,* for much the same holds descriptively. How you will choose depends, on our theory, on how it is you see things, the theory's basic principles referring to the understandings that the agent has. Principle 1 thus applies only where the propositions reporting the outcomes are *compelling* in our sense, *only where $o_{h,k}$ and $o_{h,m}$* (and whatever others there are) *report the facts they report as these are understood by the agent.* If the subjects saw the options in terms of the money involved alone, their choices indeed ran afoul of the theory. But if they saw them involving money along with (in certain cases) regret, their choices made for no trouble. Allais and also Kahneman and Tversky assume that their subjects thought in money

17 Tversky discusses this analysis in his "A Critique of Expected Utility Theory: Descriptive and Normative Considerations," *Erkenntnis* 9 (1975). It appears also in Howard Raiffa, *Decision Analysis* (Reading, Mass.: Addison-Wesley, 1968), pp. 85–6.

terms only. They offer no grounds for assuming this, and it may well be doubted.

How would Allais' two issues look without his money-terms-only assumption? One possibility is this:

Issue 1' ($=1$)

A: 1,000,000/1.   B: 5,000,000/.10
                           1,000,000/.89
                           0 + regret/.01

Issue 2

C: 1,000,000/.11   D: 5,000,000/.10
   0/.89   0/.90

Or the zero-outcome of *B* might be put as 0-when-I-could-have-had-1,000,000-for-sure. Either way, we cannot say that $u(A) > u(B)$ if and only if $u(C) > u(D)$, and so a person who follows expectedness might choose *A* and also choose *D*. Whether or not he will depends on whether his mind is on Issues 1 and 2 or on Issues 1' and 2 (or on still others). Again, how he will choose depends on the way he sees how things might come out.

Notice that zero-and-regret is not a conjunction of two distinct outcomes, no more so than zero-when-I-could-have-had-more is a conjunction of two outcomes. It is a fuller way of reporting the outcome of getting no money. (The "and" in this is adverbial only: getting-nothing-and-regretting-it is just getting-nothing-regretfully.) So the layouts of Issues 1 and 1' both report all the outcomes of *B*. But of course they report them differently, which allows for different choices being made.

Likewise with the experiments above by Kahneman and Tversky. A person might see the zero-outcome of *B* in their first experiment as 0 + regret (or as 0-when-I-could-have-had-2,400-for-sure). He might also see the 0-outcome of *B* in the second as 0 + regret (or as 0-when-I-stood-a-good-chance-of-getting-3,000). If that is how he does indeed see them, his choosing *A* and *D* may comport with our theory. And so that theory faces no challenge in the fact that many subjects chose these two options.

Let us consider another problem that yields to the same analysis. Here is Alan Gibbard's version of a scenario by Richard Zeckhauser.[18] You are being held captive by a lunatic who threatens to force you to play Russian roulette with a six-shooter that has two bullets in it. However, he offers to release you for $*m*, a very large sum: *m* is so large that you are indifferent between (*A*) paying the ransom and (*B*) pulling the trigger. Then he changes his mind, insisting instead that you must either (*C*) use a gun *four* of whose chambers are loaded or (*D*) pay $*n* to have one chamber emptied, that is, to use a gun that has *three* bullets in it. Again, *n* is such that you are indifferent between options *C* and *D*. We might put the two issues this way:

Issue 7

A: free − *m*/1.0   *B:* dead/.33
                              free/.67

Issue 8

C: dead/.67   *D:* dead − *n*/.50
    free/.33   free − *n*/.50

Since you are indifferent between *A* and *B*, $u(A) = u(B)$. By expectedness, we here get

$$u(\text{free} - m) = .33u(\text{dead}) + .67u(\text{free}). \quad (vii)$$

Let $u(\text{dead} - n) = u(\text{dead})$. Since $u(C) = u(D)$, we then have

$$.67u(\text{dead}) + .33u(\text{free}) = .50u(\text{dead}) + \quad (viii)$$
$$.50u(\text{free} - n),$$

$$.17u(\text{dead}) + .33u(\text{free}) = .50u(\text{free} - n), \quad (ix)$$

18 The Zeckhauser story appears in Kahneman and Tversky, "Prospect Theory," p. 283. Gibbard's retelling is reported in David Lewis, "Russian Roulette," unpublished.

and

$$.33u\,(\text{dead}) + .67u\,(\text{free}) = u\,(\text{free} - n). \qquad (x)$$

From *(vii)* and *(x)* together, we get $u\,(\text{free} - m) = u\,(\text{free} - n)$, which implies $m = n$. This last means that you would pay as much in one case as in the other. Yet many people would doubtless pay more for total safety than just to reduce their danger; that is, for many, $m > n$. There seems to be something wrong.

If we report the situation more fully, the problem disappears. We need to bring out how you (the captive) see the possible outcomes. Suppose you foresee that, in both issues, if you chose *not* to pay and survived, you would be glad you hadn't paid. The second outcomes of *B* and of *C* don't then appear as freedom alone but as freedom + relief (over not having paid). You are bound to prefer *B* to *C:* the odds on freedom over death are better. Since you are indifferent between *A* and *B* and between *C* and *D*, you therefore prefer *A* to *D*. And so you expect to be more relieved if you survive *C* than if you survive *B*, for you would have spared yourself the worse of the two ransoming options. This implies that $u\,(\text{freedom} + \text{relief})$ is greater in one case than in the other. If we now rewrite *(vii)* to *(x)*, we find that $u\,(\text{free} - n) > u\,(\text{free} - m)$, and thus $m > n$. Where you think only of freedom and dying and of the size of the ransoms, you are willing to pay as much in one case as in the other. But where you count the relief factor too, you will pay more for total safety.

Note that all these issues are special in that there are just two options in each. Where there are more options, things can sometimes get messier. Suppose there are three options: staking $1,000, staking $500, and staking nothing. Two gamblers both started with $1,000, staked $500, and lost it. One of them says, "Half my money is left"; the other says, "Half my money is gone." The first sees that he might have staked all he had and lost it, the second that he might have stayed home and lost nothing. For the former, the outcome is losing-500-plus-relief. For the latter, it is losing-500-plus-regret. Whether an outcome involves relief or regret (or neither) depends on which of the three co-contingent outcomes (which of the three options' outcomes in the same contingency) is the reference point used – which of them the agent takes as his base point for comparisons. This concept of people's basing points will figure in various ways in what follows.[19]

4.6 STATUS QUO ANTES

Suppose that you and a friend have gone on a trip. It has cost each of you $1,000, which each of you spent as you went along. Now that you are home again, your friend suggests that you toss a coin. If it falls heads, he will give you $1,000. If it falls tails, you will give him $1,000. Will you agree to the deal?

Take now a second situation. Some months before you went on that trip, your friend gave you $2,000. He said, "I don't know how much I will need, but here is some money for my expenses. When we leave, you pay the bills. We'll settle up when we get back." You have now returned, and the costs were $1,000 for each. He suggests that you toss a coin. He says, "If it falls heads, we'll call it quits; if it falls tails, you give me $2,000." Will you accept this arrangement? If you don't, you must of course give him the $1,000 you owe him. I would be more willing to toss the coin in this case than in the other, but to some this may seem foolish. For in both cases, *not* tossing the coin means my being

---

19 An earlier version of the analysis in this section appears in my "Rationality; A Third Dimension," *Economics and Philosophy* 3 (1987). See also Richard Jeffrey, "Risk and Human Rationality," *Monist* 70 (1987), and Ellery Eells, *Rational Decision and Causality* (Cambridge University Press, 1982), pp. 39–41. For contrast, see Graham Loomes and Robert Sugden, "Regret Theory: An Alternative Theory of Rational Choice Under Uncertainty," *Economic Journal* 92 (1982), where the project is to change the formalism, to revise the expected utility index.

out $1,000 (for my own costs) and tossing it gives me an even chance of being out nothing and being out $2,000.

Kahneman and Tversky designed an experiment formally parallel to this. Again there were two situations. In one, each person was asked to assume he had just gotten 1,000 (in Israeli pounds). He was then asked to choose between getting another 500 for sure and an even chance of getting another 1,000 or getting nothing more. In the other, each subject was told to assume he had been given *2,000* and was asked to choose between *losing* 500 and an even chance of losing 1,000 or losing nothing. The two issues here might be put like this:

Issue 9

A: 500/1.0   B: 1,000/.50
                    0/.50

Issue 10

C: −500/1.0   D: −1,000/.50
                        0/.50

The majority of the people facing Issue 9 chose *A*, and the majority of the different group facing 10 chose *D*. We may infer that many people, if they faced both issues, would choose *A* and *D*. However, there seems to be something wrong, for suppose that the outcomes are put in terms of the chooser's final assets in them. Since getting 1,000 and then 500 more comes to the same as getting 2,000 and losing 500, etc., we now have

Issue 9'

E: 1,500/1.0   F: 2,000/.50
                      1,000/.50

This is the same both as Issue 9 and as Issue 10, only differently put (in terms of final assets), and 9 and 10 are thus the same too. If anyone here chose *A* and then *D*, he faced the same issue twice, and the first time chose one option, the second time the other.

How do Kahneman and Tversky account for the likely *A* plus *D* choices? They suggest that people, in choosing, focus not on the total final positions but on the gains or losses their actions might generate for them: "The apparent neglect of a bonus that was common to both options [the 1,000 in one issue and 2,000 in the other] . . . implies that the carriers of value or utility are changes of wealth, rather than final asset positions that include current wealth."[20] They also suggest that the value curve for money is roughly S-shaped, that it goes through the origin, is generally concave for gains, generally convex for losses, and steeper for losses than for gains.

These two theses together imply that where, as in Issue 9, a person must choose either a gain for sure or a chance of gaining and these options have the same money expectation, he is risk-averse, and that where, as in Issue 10, he must choose either a loss for sure or a chance of losing with the same money expectation, he is risk-inclined. Also that I am risk-averse in the first of my vacation stories (though that offers no gain for sure) and am risk-inclined in the second. Also that the common reading of the cases in the preceding section is false: the bias in them toward certainty reflects only their nonzero payoffs' being gains. The theses imply that if these payoffs were losses, their numerical values as now, the opposite choices would have been made.

There is an alternative to this analysis, and Kahneman and Tversky brush shoulders with it. They preface their report of the experiment just cited by saying, "We now show how choices may be altered by varying the representation of outcomes."[21] Here it isn't a matter of outcomes versus final asset positions but of different presentations of the outcomes. The authors make no allowance for this in their theory of action. Nor do they think it can be used to rescue their subjects' rationality, for they hold that a sensitivity to presentations marks a failing of its own. A person who changes as the presentations change (where he

20 "Prospect Theory," p. 273. 21 Ibid., p. 273.

Some Applications

knows the presentations are coreportive) violates weak extensionality – Kahneman and Tversky call it "invariance." Thus he departs from what they consider essential to common sense.[22]
Our logic here is less demanding. The theory we have is strongly intensional; weak extensionality is lifted. The way the outcomes are presented may affect a person's choices if the presentations change the way he understands those outcomes. More to the point: his choices may be affected in accordance with rationality, for his new understandings may establish different expected utilities for him. Changing the way he sees the outcomes may make a different option come out the best.

Suppose that, in the problem just cited, the agent sees the outcomes in terms of his total assets in them. He sees one outcome as *winding up with 1,500,* another as *winding up with 2,000,* the third as *winding up with 1,000.* That is, suppose he sees the outcomes as they are put in Issue 9'. Then he must choose either *E* or *F* – one or the other, not both. Suppose, however, that his view of the outcomes factors out his initial resources, that he sees them as in Issues 9 and 10, as *gaining 500* or *1,000* or *nothing* and as *losing 500* or *1,000* or *nothing.* The choice of *A* may be maximizing in 9 and that of *D* may be maximizing in 10. He would then choose *A* in 9 and would choose *D* in 10, and this though (objectively) *A* is *E* and (so also) *D* is *F,* and he can't choose both *E* and *F.*

Let me put it differently. A person might see a loss of 500 that very way, as *losing 500.* Here he ignores the *status quo ante,* his having just got 2,000. Or he might bring that status quo in – into his description of that outcome. He would then see the outcome as *losing 500 of the 2,000 I just got,* which would count as a gain of 1,500. The utility he sets on this latter proposition may differ

---

22 See their "The Framing of Decisions and the Psychology of Choice," *Science* 211 (1981), and their "Rational Choice and the Framing of Decisions," in Robin M. Hogarth and Melvin W. Reder (eds.), *Rational Choice: The Contrast between Economics and Psychology* (Chicago: University of Chicago Press, 1987).

132

from that of *losing 500*. The utilities a person sets on the propositions reporting the outcomes as he sees those outcomes determine the expected utilities of his options. So the temporal width
of how he sees things – its including or not including his status
quo antes – may decide what is best for him. Notice that it isn't
a question of making the final assets or the gains or losses
central. The gains or losses are central either way. The question
is whether they are counted from *now* (as in Issues 9 and 10) or
from some earlier point (as in 9′).

This analysis is closely related to what we said about resoluteness. Ulysses (the real one), tied to the mast, saw the options he
would have had if he weren't as *reaching for bliss* and *passing it
by*. If he hadn't been tied to the mast, he would have reached for
bliss. His resolute namesake, walking the deck, saw those same
options as *shifting course* and *keeping to it*, and he therefore kept
himself to it. In speaking of an agent's being resolute, we noted
how the past can enter his view of his options and so govern his
conduct. In the preceding section and in this one, we note how
it sometimes enters his view of the *outcomes* and so (again)
affects how he acts.

One person's perspective may bring in the past where someone else's doesn't, and this is at the bottom of some bitter dis-
agreements. For instance, should there be a ban on research on
recombinant DNA? Many lives are likely to be saved in consequence of this research, but there are also people who may die
because of the work going on. Let us make some wild assump-
tions about the numbers and the probabilities. Here is one way
of putting it, with *A* as the *not*-banning option and *B* as banning:

Issue 11

A: not hurting anyone and	*B:* hurting 1,000,000
failing to help 1,000/1.0	and helping 1,000/1.0

It is hard to imagine anyone not preferring *A* to *B*. How then
can some people urge that this research be banned? One possible
answer is that they see the outcomes involved here differently.

Where *C* is not banning and *D* is banning, these people may be looking at

Issue 11'

C: helping 1,000,000   *D:* failing to help 1,000,000
and hurting 1,000/1.0   and not hurting anyone/1.0

They then set *D* over *C*. The obligation to help those who need it weighs with them less than the obligation to avoid hurting. That is, the positive value of helping 1,000,000 is more than offset by the negative value of hurting 1,000.

How do the two opposing groups come to their different understandings of this problem? Their difference derives from the base points that they use. The people who think in terms of Issue 11 bring in no status quo antes. They are counting from a base point of *now*. The question they ask about the new options is how many people would be made better off by them and how many worse, *relative to their circumstances, including their prospects, with the research in progress.* (So the good and ill to be yielded does not count under *A;* the *not-banning* option cannot offer what is already on its way.) Those who see things as in Issue 11', count from a point just before the work started. They think of people as helped or hurt *relative to their circumstances at that point.* In effect, their question is how many people would be made better and how many worse off *relative to what their circumstances would have been if no work had been done.*

Whether we take in some status quo ante – whether our base point is *now* or *then* – has to do with how we here see things. It has to do with whether the propositions that express how we see the outcomes involved refer to what happened or started at some earlier point. Where the base point *is* in the past, the status quo ante that is "taken in" is the period or the situation holding between that point and now. In an issue of helping or hurting, what we take in often settles things for us. To help a person is to make him better off than he now is or was at some point. To hurt him is to make him worse off than he now is or then was.

134

So the location of our basing point makes for different help/hurt statistics, and that can be decisive.

Take the million people whose lives the DNA work may save; counting from today, from a base point of *now*, stopping this work would hurt them. It would deprive them of the chance of a longer life that the work had given them. But counting instead from before that work started, stopping it only declines to help them. It can't make these people worse off than back then, before any work had been done. (Compare: is a doctor who gives up on a patient hurting him or only ceasing to help him – is he killing him or letting him die? This too depends on our basing point.)[23]

Again, to bring in the status quo ante is to see the outcomes a certain way, in terms of what happened or started in the past. It may be well to stretch the word "past" to cover the actions we have at issue (to let the word "now" refer to the moment right after we will have acted, to let the past be the *outcomes'* past). For sometimes we see an outcome in terms of our taking the action that leads to it, or of our taking that *sort* of outcome. Our having taken that (sort of) action is then itself the status quo ante we are keeping in mind. This happens most often where the action has some special moral aspect. The outcome then is colored for us by that aspect of what will yield it.

Suppose that Jack and Jill are quarreling over which of them owns some object. They both have an equal claim on it, and it can't be divided between them. They ask you to step in and settle this. Having decided to toss a coin, you now consider two options. You might (*A*) give the item to Jack if the coin falls heads and give it to Jill if it is tails, or you might (*B*) give it to Jack if it is heads and also if it is tails. Here you face

Issue 12
A: Jack/.50   B: Jack/1.0
Jill/.50

23 I have here adapted an analysis by Stephen P. Stich; see his "The Recombinant DNA Debate," *Philosophy and Public Affairs* 7 (1978).

You also notice that you might (C) give the item to Jill if the coin falls heads and to Jack if it falls tails or (D) give it to Jill come what may, this making for

Issue 13

C: Jill/.50   D: Jill/1.0
Jack/.50

How are you going to choose? You might prefer A over B in Issue 12 and C over D in 13 and choose on that basis – many people would. But then it seems you would violate expectedness. The argument is this: in order for a preference of A over B to be maximizing, it would have to be that

$$.50u\,(\text{Jack}) + .50u\,(\text{Jill}) > u\,(\text{Jack}) \quad \text{and so} \qquad (xi)$$

$$u\,(\text{Jill}) > u\,(\text{Jack}). \qquad (xii)$$

In order for C over D to be maximizing, it would have to be that

$$.50u\,(\text{Jill}) + .50u\,(\text{Jack}) > u\,(\text{Jill}) \quad \text{and so} \qquad (xiii)$$

$$u\,(\text{Jack}) > u\,(\text{Jill}). \qquad (xiv)$$

We can't have both (xii) and (xiv). It turns out that fairness (procedural equity) and expectedness do not mix.[24]

We can here set this aside. There need be nothing wrong in choosing A in 12 and C in 13. A person who chooses these options is likely to see them in a special way, to see B and D as *being unfair* and A and C as *fair*. He is thus led to see the outcomes too in terms of their fairness or lack of it, in terms of the moral shape of the options whose outcomes they would be. The outcome of B presents itself to him not as *Jack wins* but as *Jack wins where I acted unfairly*. The outcome of D he sees as *Jill wins where I acted unfairly*. The outcomes of A and of C he sees as *Jack*

24 An argument to this effect appears in Peter Diamond, "Cardinal Welfare, Individualistic Ethics, and Interpersonal Comparisons of Utility: Comment," *Journal of Political Economy* 75 (1967). See also John Broome, "Equity in Risk Bearing," *Operations Research* 30 (1982).

(*Jill*) *wins in a fair proceeding.* There are only two possible outcomes: Jack's winning and Jill's winning. But, for a morally scrupulous person, two possible status quo antes enter: his having acted fairly and his having acted *un*fairly. The utilities of *four* propositions thus figure, and so the (*xi*)-to-(*xiv*) argument fails (strictly, it doesn't apply). Where we see things in terms of fairness, we can choose fairly without violating expectedness.[25]

A closely related case is this. The indivisible good is some unit of medicine. You think it more likely to help Jack than Jill – or suppose that Jack is a friend and Jill a total stranger. You then prefer Jack's getting it to Jill's, which suggests that the expectedness of *B* is greater for you than that of *A*. Yet you may want to toss that coin, that is, to bring about *A*. What could be in your mind?

You may again be seeing the outcomes not as *Jack* (*Jill*) *gets the medicine* but in terms of being fair. Still, you needn't now see them that way. It may be that what strikes you instead is the presumption of your deciding which of two others will live. Perhaps you hold that an issue like that ought to be left to nature or to chance, that it is wrong to play God. You then see the outcomes not in terms of fairness but rather of *agency:* you see the outcomes of *A* as *Jack* (*Jill*) *gets the medicine, having been picked by chance* and the outcome of *B* as *Jack gets the medicine, having been picked by me.* The expected utility of *A* could here be greater for you than that of *B* and tossing a coin could make good sense. Notice that, in this case too, your view of the outcomes takes in what preceded (where that includes the actions that yield them).[26]

People will often differ on whether to take the past into account (and if so, then how much of it). Indeed, a person himself

---

25 I am indebted to Philip Pettit here; see his "Decision Theory and Folk Psychology," in Michael Bacharach and Susan Hurley (eds.), *Foundations of Decision Theory* (Oxford: Oxford University Press, in press).

26 The medicine case and its "agency sensitivity" analysis are Amartya Sen's; see his "Rationality and Uncertainty," *Theory and Decision* 18 (1985).

may vary from situation to situation. He may favor the Issue 11 reading of the research-banning problem and yet go along with Kahneman and Tversky in putting both 9 and 10 as 9'. If so, he reports the outcomes in the DNA case from a base point of *now* and reports the outcomes in Kahneman and Tversky's experiment by working out the asset changes from some earlier point (before he got the 1,000 or 2,000). People will often differ, and they may vary from issue to issue, but some stand must always be taken. The basing point must either be *now* or some point in the past. In money issues, the question is whether the costs already paid are *sunk*, whether the benefits collected are *absorbed* – whether what's done is done, whether the bygones are bygones. Are we now starting from scratch, or are our earlier gains and losses (or *certain* earlier gains and losses) part of our ongoing project? The answer may depend on the project, on how we are making that money.[27]

Even valuation in a life-and-death issue presupposes a basing point. A person offered a dangerous job usually worries about his life. His basing point is his moment of birth: I am alive, I might get killed, that would be a great loss. Still, this accounting is not self-evident. Suppose that some weird ideology has led him to think his life not his own. He might then not see his dying as any real deprivation. His basing point would be *now*. He might say: I have nothing to lose. I wouldn't be any worse off dead than I was before I was born.

Some stand must always be taken; our basing point has to be *here* or *there*. What if someone asks where his base point *should* be on some occasion? Our theory is neutral on that topic. It speaks of an agent's understandings in a way that allows any base-point selections. It does not say how things should be seen,

27 W. H. McGlothlin takes the increase of betting on racetrack long shots at the end of a day as a sign of the bettors trying to offset their losses – bygones aren't here bygones; see his "Stability of Choices among Uncertain Alternatives," *American Journal of Psychology* 69 (1956).

but only notes that seeings can differ, and that a difference can matter.

4.7 STATUS QUO POSTS

The understandings a person has affect what he will do, so to make sense of what someone does, we must consider his understandings. Let us look at a last class of cases.

The prototypical instance here is the Newcomb problem.[28] Suppose that two boxes are put before you and that you must take just the first one or both. The second box contains $100. The first contains either $1,000,000 or nothing, depending on how the wealthy stranger who is making the offer foresaw you would choose. If he thought you would take both boxes, he put nothing in the first box. If he thought you would take the first only, he put in the million dollars. The stranger is known to have special powers, and you think it is very probable that, whatever you do, he foresaw you would do it.

So the situation is this. If you take both boxes, there is a low probability you will get $1,000,100 and a high probability you will get $100. If you take the first one only, there is a high probability you will get $1,000,000 and a low probability that you will get nothing. Let the two-boxing option be A and let one-boxing be B. When we put numbers for "high" and "low," we might get

Issue 14

A: 1,000,100/.01	B: 1,000,000/.99
100/.99	0/.01

---

28 This first appeared in Robert Nozick, "Newcomb's Problem and Two Principles of Choice," in Nicholas Rescher et al (eds.), *Essays in Honor of Carl G. Hempel* (Dordrecht: Reidel, 1969). There are many variants; there is even one designed to induce the religious to pray – see Donald M. MacKay, *Science, Chance, and Providence* (Oxford: Oxford University Press, 1978), pp. 53–60.

Though it is clear that *B* (one-boxing) has the greater expectedness here, people divide on what they would do. Many insist that they would choose *B*, others are firmly for *A*. The *A*-choosers (two-boxers) are not being careless; they have not added things wrong. They persist even after the case for choosing *B* is spelled out for them. Can any sense be made of this?

Those who would opt for *B* suggest sometimes that what moves the others is the *dominance* of *A*, the fact that, whatever is in that first box, they would be richer by $100 if they took the second too. They go on to note that dominance cannot properly settle things here, that dominance is decisive only in contexts of probabilistic independence, where its directive has to agree with that of the expected utilities. The *A*-choosers are moved to *A* by dominance though the expected utilities point them to *B*. So they are not being rational. Or at least, that is the argument.

Still, it may be that expectedness points the *A*-choosers to *A*, not to *B*, this because they see things differently from the way laid out in 14. Notice that though they will get the contents of that first box, whatever they are, their getting this or that from that box isn't now up to them. It won't be what they had brought about – the stranger will have arranged it. This connects with the familiar thesis that only what would be brought about bears in a proper way on choice, that only the *causal effects* of an option are its proper outcomes. Again, the two-boxers' getting the contents of that first box won't be an outcome of what they did, but just a nice (or null) extra bonus. The outcomes of the two options they have are *getting $100* for one and *getting nothing* for the other. If a person sees the outcomes solely in terms of these basic payoffs, he may be looking not at 14 but at

Issue 14'

C: 100/.01	*D:* 0/.99
100/.99	0/.01

In this, *C* is two-boxing and *D* is one-boxing, and the two outcomes of *C* are the outcomes of two-boxing in the context of box

1's being full and in the context of its being empty, and so too under *D*. (Here we write *"x/y"* as short for "getting *x* in context *k* with the probability *y*.") Since the expected utility of *C* is greater than that of *D*, two-boxing can be rationalized. This is not all there is to it. Suppose we agree to reason only in terms of the brought-about effects. These needn't be put as in 14', in that most circumscribed way. They might be reported so as to also cover what would happen if the actions were taken *but wouldn't then happen because of this.* The outcomes would still be the causal effects, but we would describe them more fully.[29] The first outcome of *C* of Issue 14' might be reported as getting $100 *along with $1,000,000 that had been waiting in box 1;* the second could be reported as getting $100 *when box 1 was empty.* The first outcome of *D* could be reported as getting nothing on one's own *along with $1,000,000 from box 1,* the second as getting nothing on one's own *when box 1 was empty.* This would return us to the way we first put it, to *A* and *B* of Issue 14.

Whether or not we restrict proper outcomes to causal effects turns out not to matter.[30] The outcomes can still be differently reported, and this provides for different choices and actions. But that is then just the point. For people who see the outcomes in the more narrow of our two ways (the Issue 14' layout), the expected utility of two-boxing is greater than that of one-boxing. The reverse is true for people whose view of the outcomes is the more inclusive (as in Issue 14). And this even where we grant that only an action's causal effects are its outcomes: which of the box choices would be rational depends on how the chooser understands those effects.

---

29 The possibility of such redescriptions is remarked on by Isaac Levi; see his "A Note on Newcombmania," *Journal of Philosophy* 79 (1982). However, the moral that Levi draws is very different from mine.

30 Here I am turning against a position that used to be my own; see my *Having Reasons* (Princeton: Princeton University Press, 1984), esp. pp. 54–7. I am also going against much of causal decision theory. See David Lewis, "Causal Decision Theory," *Australasian Journal of Philosophy* 59 (1981); also Ellery Eells, *Rational Decision and Causality.*

Some Applications

Much the same analysis provides for the other scenarios of the Newcomb sort. Consider R. A. Fisher's conjecture that smoking itself does not cause cancer but that whatever does cause cancer also makes you want to smoke – hence the correlation between smoking and cancer.[31] The only causal effect of smoking is the pleasure it yields you. Let A be smoking and B be *not* smoking. We then have

Issue 15
A: some pleasure/1.0 B: no such pleasure/1.0

Clearly, a sensible person would smoke.

Most people reject this analysis; they think it is near-sighted. If you indulge your desire to smoke, you are likely to have your pleasure in the context of cancer. If you don't, you will forfeit the pleasure, but (one may hope) in a context of health. Suppose you in fact see the outcomes this way. The smoking problem now looks very different. Let C be smoking and D be not smoking and make up some probabilities, and you now see the problem as

Issue 15'
C: pleasure amid health/.01 D: no pleasure amid health/.99
pleasure amid cancer/.99   no pleasure amid cancer/.01

The outcomes here, as above, in 15, are the effects of smoking and of not smoking. They are only reported more fully, in terms of their possible contexts. If you maximize expectedness here, you are likely to wind up not smoking; the utilities you set on the outcomes so seen are likely to get you to stop. Again, which course is best for a person depends not just on his probabilities and utilities but also on how he sees the outcomes.

31 R. A. Fisher, "Cigarettes, Cancer, and Statistics," in *Collected Papers of R. A. Fisher*, Vol. 5 (Adelaide: University of Adelaide Press, 1974). A similar story appears in Brian Skyrms, *Causal Necessity* (New Haven: Yale University Press, 1980), pp. 128–9.

Or take Gibbard and Harper's fantasy of King David's lust for Bathsheba.[32] David wants her badly, but he wants even more to stay king, and he thinks that, if he called her, his people would rise against him. They wouldn't rebel because he had called her but because of his lack of a true kingly nature, a lack he believes prompts rulers like himself to abuse their female subjects. The flaw in his makeup that caused him to call her would lead the others to lose patience with him, and he can't tell whether he has the flaw except by how he now acts toward women – calling Bathsheba would make it very probable. The only effect of the summons itself is that she would come, etc. Still, this might then end in a way that would spoil the pleasure for him.

Ought a sensible king to ignore the probability of his being dethroned? The case is formally just like Fisher's. (Let *A* and *C* in Issues 15 and 15′ be calling Bathsheba and *B* and *D* be *not* calling her, and put dethroning in place of getting cancer.) What is the rational thing to do? That depends on how the outcomes are in fact seen or understood, on whether the king understands the outcomes in the broader or the narrower way.

What can be learned from the Newcomb problem and these variants of it? It seems to me that the basic message connects with that of the preceding section. There we saw that people may differ regarding the relevance of some status quo ante, the relevance of what happened or started at some time in the past. The Newcomb case now makes the same point about the status quo *post*, about what the ambient situation would be when an action came to fruition, what would then obtain or hold apart from the effect that the action had. The status quo post is the uncaused setting of a brought-about (causal) outcome, its what-would-have-been-independently setting. How should the outcomes in the Newcomb problem be reported? Should we let the foregones be foregones? Or should the way that we see these

32 See Alan Gibbard and William L. Harper, "Counterfactuals and Two Kinds of Expected Utility," in C. A. Hooker et al (eds.), *Foundations and Applications of Decision Theory*, Vol. 1 (Dordrecht: Reidel, 1978).

outcomes take in the status quo posts? I am suggesting that the one-boxers (and nonsmokers and nonsummoners) say *yes*, the contexts *should* be taken in, and that the two-boxers (and the smokers and summoners) say *no*, and that the difference in how they act turns on their stands on this matter.

The status quo ante of an outcome never in fact involves the whole past. The agent picks some point in time and keeps his mind to this side of it. He takes in the status quo ante by seeing the outcomes in terms of some situation that held between that point and now (e.g., his having been given $2,000). Likewise with a status quo post: this is never in actual practice the total later context. It is what is within some boundary the agent has drawn for himself. Taking in a status quo post means seeing an outcome of some option in terms of the situation that boundary would enclose if the option were taken (e.g., there being $1,000,000 in the box).

A person might see the possible outcomes *sub speciae aeternitatis* and *infinitatis.* He is more likely to confine his perspective in some way, to take in less of the setting. In the limit of such a confinement (as in Issues 14′ and 15), the status quo posts don't enter at all: the setting isn't considered. This is much the same as with our picking a basing point in the past. Some stand must always be taken, but the outcomes can be seen either broadly or narrowly or some way in between, though here (with the future) it is better to speak not of *points* but of basing *contours* or *frames.* Some frame is always involved, but the tightness of the frames may vary.[33]

Again, this is true not in money issues only (like Newcomb's) but in every issue we face. In real-life, non-money cases, we often take a narrow view. Our basing frames fit tightly around the outcomes of the options we have. We exclude much (sometimes all) that we know will hold independently of what we do.

---

33 The terminology of "framing" is Kahneman and Tversky's; see the works cited in note 22. But see also Erving Goffman, *Frame Analysis* (New York: Harper & Row, 1974).

But sometimes too we bring in more – we go by some larger picture. And there may here and there be people who bring in all that they know. Take a person who burns with the knowledge that, whatever happens, he will die in the end. Such a person may see all the outcomes framed in a very inclusive way. He may come to see what he does as only made of sand, to see it all as in vain. He may see every outcome *o* as *o and then one day I die*. A person who frames every outcome this way may not care what he does.

Let me concede that the framing concept is a blunt instrument for us. Compare it with the idea of a base point at some time in the past. Temporal boundaries raise no problem; every moment divides what follows from what came before. Thus it is that status quo antes can be sharply defined (e.g., the period after yesterday midnight, or after the war, or after Reagan's election) and we can exclude from our thinking all that happened before any point. But can one speak of *non*temporal boundaries of events and situations? Can events and situations be located in space in any confinable way? (Where exactly was Kennedy killed? Was it in Dallas? in Texas? on Earth?) Events and situations don't have spatial outlines, and having no outlines, they can't be framed. What we say about tight or loose frames thus cannot be taken literally.

Framing is a metaphor, and how to cash it out is unclear. I will let others think about that. Suppose that someone ate some spoiled food and that it made him sick. His getting sick is the causal effect, but this can be put in different ways. *His getting sick* (or *his getting sick to his stomach,* or *his getting intensely sick*) takes in just the effect itself. *His getting sick while playing Hamlet* takes in some of the status quo post. It refers to his playing Hamlet, which wasn't caused by his eating that fish – the basing frame is looser. *His getting sick while playing Hamlet before an audience of thousands* takes in still more. The frame around that same effect is a bit looser yet. However we spell the metaphor out, there is certainly something in it, and that is enough for us here.

Some Applications

Let me note a complication, or it may be a refinement. Leonard Savage tells this story: "A man buying a car for $2,134.56 is tempted to order it with a radio installed, which will bring the total price to $2,228.41, feeling that the difference is trifling. But, when he reflects that, if he already had the car, he certainly would not spend $93.85 for a radio for it, he realizes that he has made an error."[34] With A and C as *not* buying the radio and B and D as buying it, the car buyer's problem might be put in two ways, as Issue 16 or as Issue 16':

Issue 16

A: nothing new/1.0 B: getting a radio
for $93.85/1.0

Issue 16'

C: nothing new along D: getting a radio for
with a car I will have $93.85 along with a car
bought for $2,134.56/1.0   I will have bought
for $2,134.56/1.0

Savage holds that what a person does (or would do) in 16 should settle what he does in 16', that taking in the status quo posts ought not to make any difference. In fact, it often makes a difference in cases just like this one. People buying a raincoat often also buy an umbrella they wouldn't otherwise buy, people buying a house buy furniture they had resisted buying before, etc. On our analysis, they needn't be faulted. There need be no "error" involved.

This I have already argued. Savage disagrees, but no more of that. There remains something new to consider in his comment on the case. Speaking of a car buyer deciding 16', Savage says, "if he already had the car, he certainly would not spend $93.85

34 Leonard J. Savage, *The Foundations of Statistics* (New York: Wiley, 1954), p. 103.

for a radio for it. . . . " That is, he would not buy that radio *if the purchase of the car were behind him and he were thinking in terms of 16.* Savage infers that, if he is sensible, he won't buy the radio in 16' either. Since he would opt for *A* in 16 if the car already were bought, he has to take *C* in 16', where it isn't yet his.

I find no good grounds for saying this. Logic allows a person to choose independently in 16 and 16', whatever the dates of his purchases. Still, had that car been bought (say) last week *and this now entered the buyer's understandings,* he would be facing not 16 but

Issue 16″

E: nothing new along with a car I bought (last week) for $2,134.56/1.0

F: getting a radio for $93.85 along with a car I bought (last week) for $2,134.56/1.0

Savage's point can now be restated. It is that the agent must decide 16' as he would have decided 16″ had he been facing that issue, that he must settle *these* issues alike. If he would take *E* (or *F*) in 16″, he must take *C* (or *D*) in 16'.

The constraint this suggests is hard to pin down. We might perhaps put it this way. Suppose we are bringing some part of its setting into the view we have of some outcome. The way that we choose from among our options must reflect how we *would* have chosen had we brought in that setting's stretching to some point in time just behind us. ("Just" is exactly the problem: would the constraint still hold for these issues if "week" in 16″ were replaced by "month" or by "year"?) Another way of saying this is that the result of an s.q.-post reasoning must be the same as that of a related s.q.-ante reasoning, or rather, the same as that of a related *hypothetical* such reasoning. (The waffle word here is "related.")

This could have been put conversely too. Suppose we are bringing some prior situation into the view we have of some outcome. How we choose from among our options must reflect

how we *would* have chosen had we brought in the situation's
still holding when that outcome matures. Sameness is symmet-
rical, so the above can be turned around: the result of an
s.q.-ante reasoning must be the same as that of a related (hypothetical) s.q.-post reasoning.

It does not follow from any of this that the distinctions we
made won't hold. Our freedom is restricted a bit. Logic links our
acting, where we bring in some status quo posts, to how we
would have acted elsewhere if we there brought in certain
related antes (and again, vice versa). But the posts and antes
themselves remain distinct and separate. What is still ahead of
us is different from what is behind us; getting that car tomorrow
is different from having got it last week. And bringing posts into
our understandings is different from bringing in antes.

4.9 DOES IT WORK?

A critic has been lying in wait. He can't restrain himself longer.
"Is this what you call philosophy? You have spoken of understandings for close to 150 pages, but you have offered no proper
account, no definition whatever. It is now fairly clear to me how
you are using this concept. The applications give me a handle.
But does a cozy familiarity undo the need for analysis?"

What does this person want? He says he has got the hang
of it now. If he sees how the concept is used – how I suggest that
it *might* be used – what more could analysis do for him? Why
does he demand to have for understandings what no one ever
had for beliefs and desires? There are no proper definitions of
the concepts of these two states either. The theory of reasons
takes them in nonetheless, and we don't ask for definitions of
them, this because we know how to use them. Why should the
case for understandings be stronger?

The critic changes his line. He now rejects the whole project.
He says, "You have introduced understandings and have shown
how that concept helps. Without the new concept, the theory

leaks badly, and with it the theory floats – that is the message of this last chapter. But you give us a patched-up theory, and a patch is a sure sign of trouble. Recall the old Ptolemaic astronomy. The adding of understandings to the belief-and-desire theory is like the sewing of epicycles on orbits. Your patches are not the solution. The topic needs a Copernicus!"

Fine and good, if you can find him, but this is being too harsh. I have here added a single patch only, not many separate patches, so the analogy of the epicycles is poor. For a better analogy, think of the postulation of a new planetary body. In the early nineteenth century, Uranus was found to have an orbit departing from the one people thought it should have. The astronomer Leverrier accounted for this by inferring the existence of a distant planet, and with that new planet, Neptune, admitted, Uranus turned out to be acting just right. No one ever described the admission of Neptune as a patch-up job. So too (with all due modesty) here: the postulation of understandings lets us make sense of what is otherwise puzzling.

The critic replies, "Leave Neptune alone; that was totally different! No changes had to be made in physics to allow for the presence of Neptune. You had to tamper with basic logic to allow for understandings – you had to cut back coherence! And there is also this deeper point. Every astronomer faces the test of what the telescope finds, and the postulation of Neptune could in that test have been falsified. Nothing could ever falsify the postulation of understandings. Your theory can't ever be tested, and it therefore deserves no credence."

About my revising the basic logic: others have done this before me. We have gone over that story. We saw that expectedness was first put by Huygens in terms of monetary values, and that Bernoulli generalized the principle (revised it!) by replacing its ducats with utilities. We noted that Bernoulli's principle held only in situations of probabilistic independence, and that this prompted the introduction of conditional probabilities. The shape of the logic with which we started reflects a history of earlier efforts to square the received wisdom with practice. The grounds of the revision that I am proposing are exactly the same. About understandings not being observable: the same is true of beliefs and desires. These too can't ever be observed, not as planets are or in any other way. Nothing of consequence follows from that. The unobservability of beliefs and desires doesn't discredit the usual belief-and-desire theory. The unobservability of understandings can't discredit our theory here either.

Neither beliefs nor desires nor understandings can be observed in any way. No basis for uneasiness there, for accepted criteria exist for ascribing such states to people. The most important of these criteria have to do with what people say. If you tell me you believe it will rain and I don't think you are lying to me, I will infer that you have that belief. (The second clause speaks of what I *don't* think about you, so the question of what you believe isn't begged.) Likewise if you say that you *want* it to rain. Likewise also if you report some fact; if I don't think you are disguising how you see it, I will take the report that you give as revealing the understanding you have. So we can make the ascriptions we need, or at least sometimes we can.

Does the theory account for what happens, for how people choose and act – does the theory *work?* Does it work better than the usual theory, the belief-and-desire theory? We need to say only which works better, and that is a judgment that is easy to make. The problems we noted in this chapter have a good deal of force. The usual theory is stopped by them. Our new theory isn't, and there is nothing the old theory does that our new theory can't do. Thus our theory inherits the credit of the belief-and-desire original and gains some extra credit for serving where that theory does not.

5

SEEING THINGS RIGHT

PASCAL'S mentor in the *Provincial Letters* showed him the uses of "directing" the mind. Having a suitably directable understanding can be very convenient, for it allows us to put the rule of double aspect (double effect) to good advantage. A judge's taking a bribe is wrong, if he now sees his taking it so. But if, in his view, the money is payment, he cannot be faulted for taking it. If he will earn his pay, he deserves it.

Another case: the arsonist. Burning down the house was wrong, that is, the arson so-reported was wrong. But suppose that you asked him to do it. If he saw setting that house on fire as doing you a favor, he is in the clear. No one can be blamed for doing people favors.

Pascal found this maddening, but what was it that made him so angry? He may have held that a bribe was a bribe and that arson was arson, no matter how they were seen, that how an arsonist sees his arson makes no moral difference. If that was his line, he was being too hard. Our seeings or understandings are part of our reasons, and our reasons must bear in some way on the status of what they move us to do, on whether those doings are right or wrong. Still, perhaps what he meant was this, that how a person sees what he does is itself subject to censure. There are wrong ways of seeing things as well as wrong ways of acting. If a person is seeing things wrong, that alone is a mark against him. A judge who sees a bribe as a payment has a flawed view of what he is doing. His mind is not properly on it. In their

151

mental redirectings of others, the Jesuits misfocused their minds.

This returns us to an issue we have put off several times. Some seeings are said to be right and others are said to be wrong. In Pascal's case, there may be agreement: the monk got everything wrong. But we have noted some cases too on which people's judgments will differ. Was Orwell right to see the Fascist as a "fellow creature"? Was Rubashov right to see his confession as a service to the Party? How much of the status quo ante belongs in the report of the outcomes of some option? How much of the status quo post? The answers that satisfy some people will be resisted by others.

There are those who don't want any answers because they reject these questions. They deny that one can speak of the rights and wrongs of understandings except insofar as the judgments involved refer to coherence or some current practice. They are content to ask how an understanding advances the agent's purposes. Or they may ask how it squares with our own or with social custom, whether the understanding is widely shared, or is the sort that most people have, or the sort accepted by people in some group to which the agent belongs. They can then say about the monk that we don't see things his way, or that he was out of the mainstream, that the people of his day didn't see things as he did. They cannot say (and don't want to say) that there was something wrongheaded about him.

This position has its attractions. It promotes a certain respect for the perspectives of others. It proposes our staying receptive to a variety of points of view. Also, it offers to spare us the burden of the issue we now are facing. Still, its very attractiveness should make us a bit uneasy with it. Sure enough in some cases: is the glass half empty or is the glass half full? Did the Democrats win the election or did the Republicans lose? Was the union of West and East Germany a union of two countries or a reunion of one? Either view could be taken on these. But what about the more troubling cases? Can a mass extermination of the enemy be seen as a pacification program? Even those on the peace-bringing side may reject this report of what they brought. Have they no grounds for rejecting it other than local custom? No-seeings-are-wrong is a fallback position. We may, in the end, have to settle for it, but let us not do that here. Let us ask what sense might be made of the likely judgment that the monk saw things wrong, what sense might be made of Rubashov's struggle to get the right view of confessing, etc. And let us ask also what price we would pay if we made no headway with this and yet still thought some seeings right and others wrong (and still others neutral) – what cost there would be to our theory. How would our theory of reasons suffer if we continued to speak of right seeings but couldn't say in what rightness consisted, what made a right seeing or understanding right?

Again, we will take it for granted here that understandings can be right or wrong, that they are in this respect too like beliefs and desires. Some beliefs are right (or sound), other beliefs are wrong. Some desires are right (or proper), others are wrong (or bad). Here we meet issues different from those we met in the earlier chapters. What beliefs would be right for a person independently of what else he believed? *Correct* beliefs, yes, of course; but when is a belief correct? And what desires would be right for a person placed here or there in the world, a person, say, with opportunities like ours? These two are very old questions, as much discussed today as ever. The corresponding question about understandings has had only little attention. Indeed, it is seldom raised.

In part, this has to do with the usual neglect of understandings themselves. But even those thinkers who do not neglect them try to evade the question of their rightness. Aristotle does it by definition. For him, an agent's minor premise reports his "grasp" or "understanding" of some option, but also, understandings *must* be right; they wouldn't be understandings if they were wrong. "Understanding is identical with goodness of understanding, men of understanding with men of good understanding."[1] The idea of understandings that this proposes is not quite the same as ours, which doesn't have rightness built into it. If we went over to the Aristotelian idea, we would need a new word for seeings that misrepresent the facts, and yet another for seeings *tout court*, seeings independent of whether they present things correctly: we would need "seeing$_2$" and "seeing$_3$." Our question would then come up again. When are the facts being misrepresented – when are they being seen$_2$? Or instead, when are we seeing$_3$ them wrongly and when might we properly see$_3$ them as we do?

Another way around the question proposes that understanding is a natural faculty, that it is like, say, digestion. There are no right and wrong ways of digesting, only the way it is normally done and lapses of various sorts from that norm. There is no *should* of the matter. And this is just as well, for digestion cannot be taught; either your body can do it or it can't. Here is Kant on understanding, which he refers to as "judgment": "judgment is a peculiar talent which can be practiced only, and cannot be taught. It is the specific quality of mother-wit, and its lack no school can make good."[2] Either you have it or you don't.

Kant also puts his point differently, that the special talent is that of making *right* or *proper* judgments. He speaks of judgment as the application of rules – as the grasping or shaping of facts to which our laws (the rules) might apply – and he holds that "the power of *rightly* employing them," of rightly applying them, is a "natural gift."[3] An exercise of this natural power yields a right judgment by definition. (Kant is here joining with Aristotle.) The difficult problem is with us still. It is to distinguish what is and what isn't an exercise of this power. When is a person judging correctly? When is he seeing things right? On that we still have no clue. For this is just the question I said has hardly ever been raised.

1 *Nichomachean Ethics*, 1143a.
2 *Critique of Pure Reason*, A133, B172.   3 Ibid., emphasis added.

"Hardly ever" doesn't mean "never." A special case of the question appears in Nelson Goodman's "new riddle of induction."[4] Suppose that a hundred marbles, all of them blue, have been drawn from an urn; the next to be drawn will very likely be blue. All the drawn marbles were also *bleen*, a bleen marble being one that is either drawn before tomorrow and is blue or is drawn after and is green. Parity of reasoning suggests that the next marble is likely to be bleen, but this says that if it is drawn after midnight it is likely to be green and so *not* likely to be blue. Formally identical inferences from the same evidence put in different ways give us contradictory conclusions. We avoid the contradiction by rejecting the bleen-descriptions. But what is our warrant for rejecting them? What makes these descriptions improper?

Goodman develops an answer in terms of the record in prior inferences of the basic words involved (of the words "blue" and "bleen"). Whether or not this approach of his works, its focus is very narrow. It deals with a special question only. It has to do just with what descriptions are proper for inferential purposes – not with right seeings in general, but with right seeings in inference only. The general question remains: when is a description, in any context, proper? When are we seeing things right?

5.2 DISHONESTY

Let me turn the question around. When is a person *not* seeing things right? What are *wrong* understandings? Perhaps the answer has something to do with the motives of misrepresenting. In each of Pascal's Jesuitical cases, the agent is offered wrongheadedness. He is invited to put a new (and wrong) understanding for the one that he has. What would tempt him to do it? Suppose he adopted the new understanding. How would he be better off?

4 See his *Fact, Fiction, and Forecast*, 4th ed. (Cambridge, Mass.: Harvard University Press, 1983), pp. 72ff.

We are not speaking of situations in which the agent only pretends to rethink; there he reports some matter or other as he doesn't now see it. Take the judge who describes some money he was given as a payment for services. He is likely to see it as before, as an incentive to favor who gave it – that is, as a plain bribe. The point of the pretense is clear. The judge describes the affair as he does in order to get others to see it so, or at least to get them to think that he himself now sees it that way. He hopes in this manner to avoid their censure. No question about his purposes here.

The question is what his purpose might be where he isn't pretending. Often the answer is closely related. The judge who in fact sees the bribe as a payment wants to avoid having to censure himself. He wants to look good in his own eyes, whatever the others may think. Formally put, the situation is this. He expects to do x (to take some money). He believes that h and k are propositions coreportive of x (h is *I accept a bribe* and k is *I accept payment for services*). He does not approve of actions reported as x is reported in h but approves of these same actions reported in terms of k. He wants to feel good about himself. He has therefore got himself to understand x in terms of k.

Here is a kind of self-persuasion, though not the kind noted in Section 4.2. The agent isn't getting himself to do what he otherwise wouldn't have done (as was the case with Rubashov). He isn't adopting an understanding that might now move him out of some quandary. He isn't in any quandary at all. He wants to do x and expects that he will. The self-persuasion here is this: he is getting himself to approve what he otherwise would not approve.

Take the case of the arsonist. If he sees his job as we do, as setting some person's house on fire, he may balk at doing it. But let him give it more thought. If he gets himself to see it as a duty imposed by friendship – or as his part of a business contract, or as revenge or retaliation – he will feel better about it.

Take a more common case too. Most of us are uneasy with lying, with what we see as disguising the truth. It often comes much easier to us when we see it as a professional service, or as a concern with the feelings of others or a pursuit of some larger good. So where we know we will wind up lying, we prepare our conscience for it. We arrange to see that lie in some acceptable way.

Again, there is no issue here of what we will in fact do: we will do *x* and we know it. The point is to put a good face on that action, to find a face for us to approve when we look into the mirror. Persuading ourselves to adopt an understanding on just this basis is a self-*delusion* (the analogue for understandings of a doxastic self-*deception*). It is a public relations stunt pulled by us on ourselves. An understanding contrived for this purpose might be said to be *inauthentic*. Or we might call it *dishonest*.

This can now be extended. In the basic case above, we expect to do *x* and take a new view of that. We get ourselves to see the action so that it brings no censure on us in our own moral judgment. But change the format a bit. Perhaps someone else will do *x*, and we don't want to find fault with this person. Or perhaps he did it already and we now want to exonerate him. Or perhaps we are looking back and feeling uneasy about something we did. Understandings contrived in such cases to block our own censure are like those above. They too might be labeled *dishonest*.

There is no shortage of instances; here is one to boggle the mind. Franz Grassler, a former Nazi commissioner of the Warsaw ghetto, is speaking to Claude Lanzmann in the documentary *Shoah*. Grassler describes his official activities as "maintaining the ghetto." Lanzmann objects to the phrase. Five thousand people died every month – one cannot speak here of "maintenance." Grassler insists on the way that he put it. "But people were dying in the streets. There were bodies everywhere," says Lanzmann. "That was the paradox," Grassler replies.[5] When Lanzmann says that the ghetto served only to prepare those in it for being killed, Grassler denies having known this then. He knew it of course when he spoke with Lanzmann, and yet he still firmly held to the view that he had been "maintaining the ghetto."

One can guess why he stuck to this. It is likely he saw very early that the ghetto was just a holding pen, that he was involved in the management of an elaborate killing operation. It may be too that at some point or other he became uneasy with this. Getting himself to see what he did as "maintaining the ghetto" let him avoid self-censure. This understanding of his was dishonest, but honesty was a virtue he could not afford. He wanted to put the past behind him. There was no way that he could have done that if he still saw he was an accomplice to killers.

5.3 INATTENTION

A wrong understanding that someone has is sometimes a means of evasion. It replaces an understanding he then wants to deny. The strategy needn't be conscious, and works most smoothly where it is not. Misrepresenting here serves the purpose of helping the agent look clean to himself. Still, that cannot be central to it; this purpose of certain wrong understandings can't be what makes the understandings wrong. The same self-serving motivation could prompt an understanding that is in fact right. And besides, there are misrepresentings that are in no way purposeful.

Goodman's examples are cases in point (no purpose is served by seeing marbles as bleen), but we will keep to the Nazis. Suppose that my portrait of Grassler is false. Suppose that what Grassler reported to Lanzmann were not any second thoughts that he had. Let him have never seen himself involved in any

5 Claude Lanzmann, *Shoah* (New York: Pantheon, 1985), p. 183.

killing, never have seen his wartime assignment as anything but "maintaining the ghetto." The understanding he later reported would then not be delusory. So it would not be dishonest in the sense just suggested. Lanzmann would still reject it. He would still say it was a distortion, and many people would agree: honesty is not enough.

Take another case from that period, the case of Adolf Eichmann, the man in charge of transporting the Jews. During the initial period of his work, Eichmann understood what he was doing as supervising emigration and resettlement. Hannah Arendt quotes him as saying, "[I] regarded the Jews as opponents with respect to whom a mutually acceptable, a mutually fair solution had to be found. . . . That solution I envisaged as putting firm soil under their feet. . . ."[6] He knew of course that the "mutually acceptable solution" amounted to forced expulsion, that it involved the extortion of money and the confiscation of property. Still, he never saw it that way – never "envisaged" it so. The picture we have of him makes it clear that he then saw things as he later reported. He didn't contrive an understanding to replace one that made him uneasy. He was never ill at ease. If dishonesty reflects a bad conscience, he was never dishonest.

This at least is Arendt's conclusion. She subtitles her book about Eichmann "A Report on the Banality of Evil." Her point is that it is wrong to think of evil as springing from villainous urges, as inspired in every instance by the desire to destroy. The desires a villain has may be tame; viewed in isolation, they may even look good. Eichmann's wanting to arrange a "mutually acceptable solution" was itself hardly monstrous. What put it on the rails to horror was its connection with his shallow understanding, with his seeing of extortionate arrangements as "mutually acceptable solutions." Eichmann's mind was full of such slogans and fancy phrases and formulas, and these kept

---

6 Hannah Arendt, *Eichmann in Jerusalem* (New York: Penguin, 1965), p. 56.

him at a distance from the reality of what he was doing. In a later book, Arendt sums up, "There was no sign in him of . . . specific evil motives, and the only notable characteristic one could detect . . . was something entirely negative: it was not stupidity but *thoughtlessness.* "[7]

The source of the special evil in Eichmann was his distorted understanding, and this had to do with his thoughtlessness, with what Arendt also calls *inattention.* His mind dealt in foggy slogans. He never saw through them to things as they were. Arendt's account of Eichmann recalls the Platonic philosophy of knowledge by acquaintance. This holds that all knowledge involves an encounter, a vision of things as they are, and also that knowledge makes for virtue, that "goodness is connected . . . with a refined and honest perception of what is really the case."[8] A person who sees the world as it is cannot have Eichmann's fantasies. And so he cannot bring himself to act as Eichmann did.

It isn't enough to be honest, and a Platonist claims to know why: understandings are right or sound only where they rest on attention, only where things are seen as they are. This idea has some appeal, and we often pay lip service to it. We say that Orwell's eyes were opened. The mists of ideology had lifted for him. He had seen the naked truth – he had had a *revelation.* The Fascist before him was *a man;* if he had fired, he would have killed a fellow human.

But metaphysics is messy business. One can do it in too many ways. The Fascist was indeed a man, but the man was also a Fascist. How was one truth more real than the other? If Orwell's captain were told of what happened, he would have said, "You

7 Hannah Arendt, *The Life of the Mind,* Vol. 1 (New York: Harcourt Brace Jovanovich, 1978), p. 4.
8 These words are the modern Platonist Iris Murdoch's in her *The Sovereignty of Good* (London: Routledge and Kegan Paul, 1970), p. 38. For Murdoch, "attention [to things as they are] . . . is the . . . proper mark of the active moral agent," p. 34.

could have killed a damned Fascist!" Some people will see it as Orwell did, others will side with the captain. But does who saw it right on that day depend on what there was to be seen?

Or let us take our more recent example. Eichmann arranged for extortionate settlements and these were mutually agreed upon – there was no choice but to agree. It took an ugly sort of perspective to call these arrangements "agreements," but, in a way, that is what they were. We are bound to condemn this view of them, to mark such thinking as a source of evil. But we can't expect metaphysics to support that judgment. What Eichmann said about his arrangements was in fact true enough. And metaphysics is even-handed; it has to endorse all truths alike, though not every truth reflects what could be a right seeing.

Are we here being too hasty? Metaphysicians sometimes distinguish *essential* from *incidental* truths. The soldier was a man in his *essence,* but only incidentally a Fascist. Eichmann's arrangements were essentially extortions and only incidentally agreements. This suggests that we see a thing rightly where we see what is essential in it. And that would bring back Plato's idea. It would mean that seeing things rightly involves attending to what they *really* are like.

But that would leave us just where we were. For what endorses this metaphysics? What warrants our positing a distinction in the world between the essential and the incidental? Only the idea that there must be something for the right-wrong seeings distinction to reflect. The new distinction can't ground the old; it does nothing but reproduce it. And of course we meet the same issues in this contrived domain. Granting the new distinction for the moment: what determines which truths are essential and which only incidental? The captain could say that his being a Fascist was a part of the essence of that soldier. There is no way of debating this matter that doesn't beg the question of how he should have been seen.

So let us put off metaphysics. The rightness of seeings can't be reduced to what is. Wrong seeings as well as right ones look to the way that things are, if the seeings grasp some fact – if the propositions that express them are true. Could we take this line instead, that every truth is equally true but that some count for more than others? The soldier's being a Fascist was as true as his being a man, but the latter was more important, at least on that day in that situation. Still, this is just another way of speaking of how it was right to see him, a way of ranking the seeings themselves. And so it too leads us back to the question of how things should be seen, of when things are seen rightly: the question with which we began.

5.4 NO PROBLEM

These ideas don't come to much, and we have little else.[9] So we have made no progress. How serious is this for us? Not very serious, I think. At least it isn't very serious if we can live without all the answers, and this we must do in any case. Let me dust off some skeletons we have in the back of our closet. They have been there from the start. The questions of the rightness of beliefs and desires came with the house we took over. There has been much discussion of them, but it has left them too without answers.

When is a belief that someone has right? I am not asking about what it means for that belief to fit in with others, or with those other beliefs of the agent's that are counted as *evidential* – or with all his beliefs and desires and probabilities and utilities. That would be a matter of its coherence with those beliefs and the rest, and we are not concerned with that now. (Our question about the rightness of understandings wasn't about their coherence either; perhaps the coherence of understandings comes to just univocity, though our provisos in Section 3.7 also bear on

9 I consider one other approach in my "Under Which Descriptions?" in Amartya Sen and Bernard Williams (eds.), *Utilitarianism and Beyond* (Cambridge University Press, 1982).

this.) A belief that fits in with everything else may be wrong nonetheless. What conditions *aside* from coherence should be set on beliefs?

We may be told that a right belief is a belief in a true proposition and that a true proposition is one that reflects or corresponds to the world. (This adapts the Platonic idea of the rightness of understandings.) What in this context is the *reflection* or *correspondence* of propositions? On one theory, it is some mapping of the components of propositions on the components of the world. Here we run into further questions. What are the components of propositions, and what are the components of the world, and also, what must the mapping be like? Despairing of this, some authors cut back. They suggest that a true proposition corresponds to a fact as one unit to another (never mind the components), but this can't help us at all – that is, we cannot make use of it. We have been taking a fact to be whatever a true proposition reports. Having identified facts from the start in terms of the concept of truth, we cannot now hope to make sense of truth in terms of the concept of facts.

Or we might give up correspondence and speak of constituence instead. We might say, with Wittgenstein, that "The world is everything that is the case"[10] and take this to mean that the world is the totality of all true propositions. (Wittgenstein makes it the totality of *facts*.) A true proposition then would be a constituent, a part (a component!) of the actual world, and that would flesh out the sought-for analysis of right beliefs as those that focus on the truth. I don't think we need quarrel with this; it gives us a neat definitional circle. But the circle is very small and little light issues from it.

Regarding the rightness of people's desires, the situation is equally dark. What makes it right to want *this* and not *that*? Here again, it isn't coherence; a desire that fits in with all the others (and with one's other mental states) may be wrong. This excludes making the rightness of desires the same as their being

10 *Tractatus Logico-Philosophicus*, 1.

rational, the same as their maximizing expected utilities, for that is an internal condition too – rationality is a sort of coherence. What other (external) condition might be set on the desires people have?

Perhaps we should look to the nature of what is wanted, to some special character of it (as we did with beliefs). But what should we then look for there? What should an object of wanting be like? Some would say that a proper desire is a desire for something *good*. But good for the agent, or good for all? And of course too, what is *good*ness? Can what is good be specified without taking note of what people want? Or is it not what people want but what they would *rightly* want that counts – which would bring us full circle? Again, these questions have a long history, but they remain as open as ever.

On all of this, we are left treading water. There is no solid ground to stand on, no external, objective basis for a judgment on beliefs and desires. Still, we don't always need solid ground. The lack of a handle on beliefs and desires – on their *rightness* – has never caused problems. It has never troubled the usual belief-desire theory of action. Why then should we be worrying here? Our having no handle on the rightness of seeings raises no problems for us either. So it can't count against our theory, a theory that makes how we see things central.

Indeed, how could it have counted? Our theory of action is a descriptive theory, a theory of what people are like. How a person *ought* to see things has no possible bearing on this. Why then did we bring up the issue? Because, as agents, we cannot ignore it. Engaged in some action, we often consider whether we should be doing what we are. Often, too, looking back on it later, we ask ourselves whether we ought to have done it. This comes down to our asking ourselves whether the reasons that moved us were sound, and so it leads us to the question of whether our understandings or seeings were right. But then, again, when *are* they right? As theorists of action we can shrug off this question, off this question, but as actors ourselves we can't.

INDEX

adoptiveness, 92–4
agency sensitivity, 137n
Allais, M., 36n, 121–6
Apel, K. -O., 70n
Aquinas, T., 63n
Arbuthnot, J., 30n
Arendt, H., 159–60
Aristotle, 7, 9–20, 55–60, 65, 80,
  112–13, 153–4
Arnauld, A., 61
Arrow, K., 98–100

Bacharach, M., 137n
basing frames, 144–5
basing points, 129, 133–8, 144–5
belief
  implicit analysis of, 39–40, 51
  principles of, 50
  rightness of, 162–4
Bennett, D., 43
Bentham, J., 38–9
Bernoulli, D., 32–4, 37, 46–7, 149
Bernoulli, N., 32
Bolker, E. D., 94–5
Borel, E., 36n
Braithwaite, R. B., 79n
Brennan, W. J., 105–7, 109
Brodrick, J., 63n
Broome, J., 136n
Buffon, G. L. L., 36n
Burtt, E. A., 38n

Cardano, G, 24–7
Carnap, R., 24, 74n
causal decision theory, 140–1
Cherniak, C., 53n
Churchland, P. M., 42n
closure, 13–14, 50, 88–9, 93–4

coherence, 46–51, 88–95
compellingness, 91–4
conflict, 102–9
consequentialism, 48, 91–3
consistency. *See* coherence
coreportiveness, 74–7
correspondence theory, 163

D'Alembert, J. L., 35–6
David, F. N., 23n, 25n, 27n
Davidson D., 17n, 43–5, 76n, 114n
Dennett, D., 52n
desires
  bottom-line, 56–8
  implicit analysis of, 39–40, 51
  principles of, 50, 65–9, 88–9, 93–4
  rightness of, 163–4
Diamond, P., 136n
dishonesty, 157–8
division problem, 27–30
double aspects, 63–5
double effects. *See* double aspects
drivenness, 14–16, 86

Edmunds, L., 15n
Eells, E., 129n, 141n
effectiveness, 15–16, 86
Eichmann, A., 159–61
Elster, J., 118n
entertaining, 77–8, 83–4
expectedness, 30–6, 40, 46–50, 87–8,
  90–5
extensionality. *See* intensionality

facts, 74–5
fairness sensitivity, 136–7
Fermat, P., 27–30
Fisher, R. A., 142–4

Index

Fodor, J. A., 42n, 53n
Fontaine, A., 34–5
Fournival, R., 22, 24

Galileo, G., 25–6
generalization, 65–9
Gibbard, A., 127–8, 143
Goffman, E., 144n
Goldman, A. I., 17n
Goodman, N., 155
Gorovitz, S., 36n
Grassler, F., 157–8

Hacking, I., 26n
Hagen, O., 36n., 121n
Harper, W. L., 143
Hippocrates, 18
Hogarth, R. M., 132n
Hooker, C. A., 143n
Horgan, T., 42n
Hume, D., 16
Hurley, S., 137n
Huygens, C., 30, 32, 149

idealization, 52–4, 100, 104
impartiality, 95
inattention, 160–1
intensionality, 95–100, 132
intention, 61–5
intentionality, 45

Jackson, F., 42n
Jeffrey, R. C., 35n, 94–5, 129n
Jesuits, 61–5, 67
Jevons, W. S., 38–9
Jonsen, A. R., 63n

Kahneman, D., 123–7, 130–3, 138, 144n
Kant. I., 7, 65–70, 154
Kendall, M. G., 23n, 27n, 29n
Koestler. A., 108
Kyburg, H. E., 37n

Lanzmann, C., 157–8
Leibniz, G. W., 24
Leverrier, U., 149
Levi, I., 46n, 109n, 141n
Lewis, D., 127n, 141n
Loomes, G., 129n

lottery problem, 36–7
Lycan, W. G., 42n

MacKay, D. M., 139n
McClennen, E. F., 117–20
McGlothlin, W. H., 138n
Machina, M., 124n
major premise, 55–9
maxims, 65–70
Menger, K., 34, 37
mentalizing, 53–4, 101
Mill, J. S., 38
minor premise, 55–60
Mischel, T., 83n
Munier, B. R., 118n
Murdoch, I., 160n
myopic choice, 117

Nell, O., 67n
Newcomb problem, 139–44
noncontradiction, 50
Nozick, R., 139n
Nussbaum, N., 11n

O'Neill, O. See Nell, O.
Ore, O., 24–5, 26n, 27n
Orwell, G., 1–3, 6, 55–6, 59, 79, 84, 88, 94, 100, 152

Page, A. N., 32n, 35n
partitions, 23–5
Pascal, B., 27–30, 32, 60–5, 151–2
Pearson, E. S., 23n
permutations, 23–6
persuasion, 105–9
Pettit, P., 42n, 137n
Peverone, G., 29
Plato, 20, 102–3, 160–1
points, problem of. See division problem
Poisson, S. D., 35n
preemptiveness, 92
Price, H. H., 78n
probability, 20–6
  conditional, 47–8
  as degree of belief, 26, 31, 38
  implicit analysis of, 39–40
  principles of, 49–51
  ranges of, 46
propositions, 71–8
provisos, 91–5

166

For EU product safety concerns, contact us at Calle de José Abascal, 56–1°,
28003 Madrid, Spain or eugpsr@cambridge.org.

www.ingramcontent.com/pod-product-compliance
Ingram Content Group UK Ltd.
Pitfield, Milton Keynes, MK11 3LW, UK
UKHW012342130625
459647UK00009B/468